Nancy Ann's Toy Fair exhibit of her well known shoe display as shown in the May, 1941, *Toys and Novelties* magazine.

Nancy Ann Storybook Dolls

Marjorie A. Miller

NANCY ANN ABBOTT

Published by 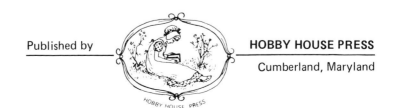 HOBBY HOUSE PRESS

Cumberland, Maryland

HOBBY HOUSE PRESS
900 Frederick Street
Cumberland, Maryland 21502

ISBN: 0-87588-156-4

Dedicated To

My Granddaughter
Karen Deanna Miller

Acknowledgements

I should like to thank all of you who have contributed to this book. I am grateful to all the contributors especially Mrs. James J. Wilson, Nancy Ann Abbott's dear friend; Louise Skoglund, who gave me needed encouragement; Mrs. Conrad (Jackie) Robertson for the help in identifying many dolls; Coriene (Corky) Jones, former secretary of Nancy Ann Dressed Dolls, Inc. whose help was immeasurable; Mrs. Ethel Junker, Mr. A. L. Rowland's sister, for her confirmation of important facts and pictures and former employees, Fay Redman, Mrs. Leo A. Scherrer, Ruth Thon, Katherine (Mellet) Koston, Betty Kelley, Mary Pardine, Irene Kowalcxyk, Elvira Brooks and Joan Haverty who were very helpful in assisting me to obtain my research material, making it possible to organize this book. Additional information was obtained from Helen P. Lowe, Ruth M. Brandon, Emma Bystron, Charles E. Kelly, Loyla Holbrock, David and Beth Redman, Flora E. Barron, Frank Blair, William Backman, George Kurrell and the doll collectors who have shared pictures of their dolls for identification purposes. I should like to thank the staff of Card & Camera Shop in Elgin, Illinois, especially Dale Gathman; Mary Buchwald of the Courier News and Esther Holtz and Evelyn Strepek for their accompanying me here, there and everywhere. Last, but most important, my husband Paul — without his patient understanding and financial support all this would have been impossible for me.

Table of Contents

Introduction

I have felt the need to write this book as a tribute to Nancy Ann Abbott, the original Nancy Ann Storybook Doll manufacturer in the United States; to her partner, Allan L. Rowland; as well as helping the many Nancy Ann doll collectors who have cherished and admired her countless outstandingly beautiful creations.

Nancy was referred to by many within her home state of California as "The Doll Lady" and her place of business as "The Doll House." Her story is one of many accomplishments, more than the average person could hope for within one's lifetime. In spite of the numerous odds against her to achieve her goals, she never failed, except for her battle against an illness later in life. This battle alone is a worthy example to each of us.

What made the "The Doll Lady" such a unique person?

Hopefully, this book will provide you with the answers. When you have read this book may you feel as I do—filled with admiration and appreciation towards her for the beauty and perfection she gave us in the form of her dolls and their clothing, and her courage and grit to face unforeseen obstacles.

May this book be helpful to all doll collectors and doll dealers who are interested in the correct identification of the Nancy Ann Storybook Dolls, informative facts regarding production and various stages of doll mold changes.

May this book also help to stop a great portion of the "guessing game" when the doll's original box or small circular gold wristband has been lost by accident or by just plain carelessness, thus the loss of its' proper identification.

Nancy Ann Storybook doll Quintuplets in their basket. Each doll is 4½ in. (11.5cm) in length, painted bisque, molded brown hair, brown eyes, slightly smiling mouth, with jointed bent limbs, the left hand is in a fist, the right hand is also closed except for the index finger which is straight. The marking on the back of doll; MADE / IN // JAPAN// 88. Each dressed in short pink organdy dress, slip, white cotton diaper, booties with pink ribbon ties. Wicker basket is covered with sheer cotton with small rose bud pattern, skirt and handle of basket is pink organdy, pink bows trim the top of skirt, a lighter pink satin ribbon is used as trim around the skirt.

I. "The Doll Lady"

Illustration 1. The Emporium display in San Francisco, CA. This photograph was used in *Playthings* , 1945.

Nancy Ann Abbott's Early Life

From a small child on Nancy Ann Abbott began to build solid ideas and goals. Though very shy by nature, she observed quite carefully all that took place about her. She was a do-it-yourself-type individual, slightly impatient for end results. Her fondness for dolls and dressing them was basic as a small child and never vanished. If she did not have a doll on hand, Nancy would improvise.

Referred to by many as "The Doll Lady," Nancy Ann Abbott's real name had been Rowena Haskin. She was born in Lake County, California, February 22, 1901. At an early time in her life her family, which consisted of her mother Edna May (Conrad) Haskin, father Archibald C. Haskin, and brother Byron (Nancy being the youngest), moved to San Francisco in the North Beach section. Mr. Haskin had previously been a school teacher; after this move to San Francisco he ventured into the commercial advertising profession. Mr. Haskin is credited with the well-remembered cover on the Albert Milling Company's pancake box — a man dressed as a chef making flapjacks over an open fire. Nancy's mother was a beautiful petite lady. She and her daughter maintained a wonderful relationship. Mrs. Haskin, though 84 years of age at the time of Nancy's death (1964), was able to supervise the care of her daughter's last days.

Shortly after the family moved to San Francisco, Mr. Haskin was killed in an automobile accident. The traumatic shock was only made tolerable for Mrs. Haskin, Nancy and her brother due to the love and supportive help given them by Nancy's grandmother and Nancy's three aunts. One aunt, Aunt Clara, remained close to Nancy throughout her lifetime.

Nancy attended the College of Arts and Crafts in Oakland, California. She was a fair artist but, at that time, her education had not encouraged her to pursue this area as her main lifetime goal. Little did she realize what a perfect foundation this knowledge would provide for her in later years.

One can only surmise if the fact that her brother, who was an excellent cameraman and later became a director in Hollywood, influenced Nancy's choice of a film career and dress designer for a short time. She worked as a dress designer for prominent actresses while awaiting roles in various movies. Nancy took part in small roles as well as lead roles in the movies, plus danced in revues. The last two films Nancy took part in were *Broadway Melody* and *42nd Street*. While on the set she would dress dolls in miniature representing costumes worn by her actress colleagues, giving them away as gifts. Her first such doll was given to Dolores Costello, reportedly an actress on the set who was a friend of Nancy's.

Nancy's enjoyment of horseback riding and playing tennis proved to be helpful in sustaining the hard work encountered when acting for a movie.Considering Nancy's shyness, one cannot help but understand her departure from filmland. The closeness of many wonderful people she met and dear friends she attained in Hollywood were remembered by her years thereafter. Actually, Nancy's name as an actress was Nancy Phipps. When leaving Hollywood Nancy changed her name to Nancy Ann Abbot. Her boundless affection for the name Ann is clearly displayed in the naming of so many of her little doll creations, as we so well have seen.

In 1935 Nancy opened a book-lending shop, reportedly named Book Lending Library Shop, on Sotter Street in San Francisco, California. This era in United States' history was quite a challenging one to the young group that gather-

1

ed in Nancy's shop. The Depression did not alter their hopes and dreams of a good lifestyle. With books in hand, many would proceed to the coffee shop nearby where lengthy discussions were conducted regarding each one's future hoped-for achievements. It was at this time that Nancy met Allan L. Rowland, called "Les" by all who knew him well. Mr. Rowland at that time was employed by the Corporation Department of the State of California. He was a very friendly, enthusiastic person and quite knowledgeable in financial matters. It has been related by many who knew him that he was an extrovert in the full meaning of the word.

As she had done previously in Hollywood, Nancy continued to dress dolls with creations she designed and sewed and began placing a few dolls here and there within the book-lending shop for the purpose of selling them. She worked at her apartment at night. There, the ironing board was always up and ready and her kiln was on hand, as was her sewing machine.

Nancy's first and most enthusiastic buyers were the girls from the Metropolitan Life Insurance Company; it was near Nancy's book-lending shop. Each sale was a delight to Nancy and encouraged her to begin to plan in earnest to establish her own company. This would be for the purpose of making beautiful outfits for small dolls, with only the best materials, just as those one would hope for within one's own wardrobe, and for the purpose of making dolls that children would enjoy, as well as attracting the attention of adults as collectibles. Many sincere friends advised her against this type of doll, stating the market would be too limited to be practical. Mr. Allan (Les) Rowland believed it was a sound plan and gave Nancy supportive encouragement and advice along business matters. Nancy left the book-lending shop after approximately eight months and was on her way to establishing the Nancy Ann Dressed Dolls Company in 1936. Later, in 1937, Mr. Rowland became a partner with Nancy's company. The company name was changed to Nancy Ann Storybook Dolls Inc., on December 26, 1945.

Nancy Ann Abbott's Private World

Regardless of the innate shyness so characteristic of Nancy's nature, her private world was a very active and stimulating one. It included many party affairs, theater events and activities relating to her hobby of the raising of orchids. She maintained her contact with actors and actresses she had known previously, and enjoyed socializing with prominent persons from all walks of life.

Nancy enjoyed horseback riding, tennis, swimming and her very favorite hobby—raising orchids. This should not be too surprising , for the fragile beauty of the orchid seemed to match the lovely way Nancy chose to bring fairy tales alive to the thousands of youngsters, as well as adults, who were lucky enough to own some of her dolls.

Her household would not be complete if it did not contain one or more pets. Cats were meaningful to Nancy. Her various dogs included two perky Pekingese named "Ming-Toy" and "Fatso." The precious little "Fatso" outlived "Ming-Toy." Her two standard-sized poodles were "Mussette" and "George;" the animals' playfulness delighted Nancy. The last little dog in her household was a miniature-sized poodle named "Gladys." We cannot forget to mention the wise parrot,"Owen."

One of the most beautiful and elaborate homes that Nancy had acquired was in Hillsborough, the part of California referred to as the "Peninsula." This house was part replica of the White House in Washington, D.C. It contained 19 rooms, of which five were large bedrooms, each having its own private bath. One bedroom was kept exclusively for Nancy's mother, regardless if she were there at all times or not. Nancy cherished her mother dearly and always cared for her. There was a time her mother helped Nancy by making the little bows for the Storybook Dolls' hair or dresses and was paid accordingly.

The living room was 48ft. (14.63m) by 30ft. (9.14m) with a Savonnerie rug. A beautiful baby grand piano also adorned this room; it had been in the White House when former President Hoover was in office. The furniture was both modern and antique. Another prize possession was her dining room set which had formerly belonged to Rudolph Valentino.

The lady who helped Nancy with the upkeep of this outstanding home was Anna Mikka. She was like a mother to Nancy. On top of all this she was talented when it came to baking goodies. A particular organization phoned once requesting a donation. Anna Mikka took the message and Nancy returned the call. A mistake was made by this organization 's representative when she referred to having spoken first to Nancy's housekeeper. That did it; no one was ever permitted to refer to "Nanna" Mikka as Nancy's "housekeeper" again. Not surprisingly, the organization did not receive a donation. That is how strongly Nancy felt Anna was a part of her family.

The picturesque three acre lawn plus garden was cared for by Mr. D. Nakumno. The large greenhouse, with its controlled temperature system, contained her precious orchids. There, white silk was used as a background for their beauty.

In 1950 Mr. Frank Blair was employed by Paooxel Pools, the company that built Nancy's swimming pool. Later Mr. Blair formed his own company and thereafter maintained the care of the pool. Nancy not only enjoyed swimming but it also provided the necessary exercise so needed for one who spent so much time sewing or at the drawing board.

There was a time that Nancy felt she truly had a living doll to care for. A couple with marriage difficulties separated, resulting in Nancy's caring for their little girl. This could be said to be one of the highlights of Nancy's happiness, having to care for this little girl. No child was ever dressed as she was with ribbons, bows and the like. After about two years, the parents reunited and Nancy was not able to retain guardianship. Though Nancy tried to maintain contact with the family there was no word from them. However when the child became a young lady and married, she did contact Nancy and visit her.

Nancy's achievements with her orchids were outstanding. One might say just this one phase of her life could be classified as a career in itself. Her appointment as a Probationary Judge was October 8, 1955, and she later became an accredited American Orchid Society Judge on October 14, 1957. During the period 1956 through 1963 she attended 45 American Orchid Society Judgings for the Society to judge orchid shows. She was active in the following: American Orchid Society, Peninsula Orchid Society and San Francisco Orchid Socity which she and Mrs. James J. Wilson founded (in fact, the first of the Society's meetings was held at "The Doll House" on Post Street in San Francisco, California).

Awards won by Nancy were: Sic Valentine var. Sunset A.M. 85 ptc., C. Pele var Haleakala A.M. 82 ptc. and Blc. Pimola var "Gimlet" 82.3 A.M., just to name a few.

I believe Nancy's life as a whole was a gratifying and happy one with many satisfactions the average person would not have the opportunity for within his or her own lifetime.

II. "The Doll House"

"The Doll House" Begins

It has been stated by one who knew Nancy's beginning well that she started her venture in 1936 with the small sum of $125 working capital, working from her apartment at first, 16 to 18 hours a day. The promotion involved with selling was not something she was well-suited for; thus the need for Mr. Allan L. Rowland, a gentleman knowledgeable in financial matters, whom she met while working at the book-lending shop. He gave her his helping hand and became her partner shortly thereafter in 1937. The Nancy Ann Dressed Dolls Corporation was incorporated February 23, 1937. It was referred to by many as "The Doll House."

The first dolls were the "Hush-a-Bye Baby" dolls with bodies made in Japan. It was also Nancy's desire to make collections of "storybook" dolls illustrating nursery tales and jingles. With encouraging sales and the return received from the same, the next step was obtaining a small shop on Howard Street in San Francisco.

By January 1939 another move had to be made to 275 Ninth St., San Francisco. An ad was placed in the paper for "Help Wanted." One outstanding person responding was Fay Redman who had been a school teacher and was out of work due to Depression repercussions. Mrs. Redman was immediately hired. The intuitiveness of Nancy's ability to know what type of person would be of the greatest help to her proved well-founded many times over in future selections of employees. Fay Redman became, in time, Nancy's right-hand lady and remained with the company until "The Doll House" was no more.

Mr. Rowland, with the help of Via Drysdale who worked at the Emporium Store at 835 Market Street, San Francisco, could be said to have been the first promotional starting point for the quanitites of orders relating to the Nancy Ann Storybook Dolls. The most popular at the beginning were Hush-a-Bye Baby, Little Bo Peep and Cinderella. Additional stores, including Marshall Field, May Company, City of Paris and Harrod's of London soon became interested. The dolls were also sold in Johannesburg, South Africa!

Illustration 2. Early photograph of Nancy Ann Dressed Dolls Corporation when it was located at 275 Ninth Street, San Francisco, California.

Greetings from our new home

Illustration 3. Located at 1298 Post Street, San Francisco, California. "The Doll House" (as many in the San Francisco area referred to it) moved to this site in 1942.

The Doll Lady opened the first doll pottery of its type in the United States in Berkeley, California. Here doll bodies and parts were made and sent to be completed at 275 Ninth Street. Once again in 1942 The Doll House was moved from Ninth Street to the corner of Post and Franklin Streets in San Francisco, due to necessary expansion resulting from mounting orders for her dolls.

A story related to me by Mr. Charles E. Kelly so typifies the ingenuity of Nancy; when she felt no one else would be able to do as well as she, she would do it herself.

A large loan had to be applied for to expand the business. Addition capital was needed for hiring more employees, buying more materials and increasing the output of dolls. She went to see Mr. Charles Kelly, a businessman, prior to this loan. At that time he was working for the Sable Bay Fur Company, 1210 Market Street, San Francisco. She explained to him there was to be a financial conference soon where she wished to make a good impression and felt a fine fur coat would certainly help. At this time in the 1930s it was difficult to obtain a loan if you were a small business and doubly hard if you were a woman. Nancy selected an ermine coat; the garment was very lovely and she looked terrific in it. "She was delighted with her choice and I was too," reflected Mr. Kelly.

However, that was the point at which the problems began, one being the necessary credit. Because Nancy had to finance the purchase, she did not have the required cash. Credit at that time in history was very hard to come by, in contrast with today's practices. Men had enough trouble getting credit; for a woman alone it was nearly impossible, with a few exceptions. Credit was rarely accepted for a woman whose job's life span was less than three years old. But this did not stop Nancy from approaching Mr. Kelly and asking for a loan. It was Mr. Kelly's company's practice to sell contracts to various finance companies, who then became holders in due course. When Mr. Kelly contacted Miss Abbott, she was most understanding. He promised to keep trying, but had no luck at all. Finally he made a decision: the store would keep the contract and she would pay the store directly instead of a finance company. This was a radical departure from the regular business practice. His boss, rather alarmed at this decision asked, "If no one else wants it, why us?"

Miss Abbott paid Mr. Kelly's company's contract in full and was never late by as much as one day. In fact, their favorable experience with Nancy caused them to reexamine their attitude toward women resulting in considerable profit to the store.

The story of Nancy's loan is a typical example of Nancy's faith in herself and her ability to convince others of the same. Helping herself by obtaining her loan made it possible for others to obtain credit at the Sable Bay Fur Company. At the same time, the Sable Bay Fur Company made a better profit, rather than discounting a "paper" of credit to another company.

At "The Doll House" on Post Street, sales grew almost out of all proportions providing employment to many. This third location at 1298 Post Street was arranged to accommodate all who worked there with as much ease and and convenience as possible. Mr. Rowland's office was on the main floor, ideal for business meetings. He made everyone welcome, providing a bar with all the conveniences at hand. It was not a prevalent matter in the early 1940s to have an office so arranged, as many are today. He had great foresight regarding successful sales.

Nancy's office was on the second floor, close to the employees. Adjacent to Nancy's office was a large room filled with bolts of beautiful material, satin ribbons, gorgeous lace, etc. - - all convenient for Nancy and the pattern cutters. Nancy worked among the cutters, sewers, dressers and artists, designing new dolls and their exquisite costumes. Every detail was an expression of her perfection. Nancy Ann Abbott was truly an artist and had such beautiful taste. When the bolts and bolts of fabric would come in, it was like Christmas for her staff to go through them and see what had been bought. Many of the laces that were used on the dresses and on the hats were imported and of the finest quality (that is just one thing that kept Nancy at the top for so many years). Her competitors could not touch her for design, quality and originality, plus her knack for combining unusual colors together for a stunning effect.

Beyond Nancy's office were the many rows of sewing machines and other equipment. Mr. William Bachman designed and built the complete conveyor system for moving the material from floor to floor. The third floor was arranged for the cafeteria. The first intention was to provide free hot lunches but, due to government regulations, this was not possible at this time. Therefore, the employees were charged only for the amount the food cost. The food was extremely good as the cook who prepared the meals was very talented. Each Christmas there was a beautiful big party with a lovely tasty turkey dinner in the cafeteria. Nancy personally chose a gift for each of the employees and then wrapped them beautifully for distribution by Santa Claus. It has been said that Nancy's and Les' roles as employers were "one in a million." All birthdays were remembered with a cake.

Illustration 4. This is the only professional photograph of Nancy Ann Abbott and her partner, Allan Leslie Rowland. *Courtesy Ethel Mae Junker, Mr. Rowland's sister.*

Loyalty To Each Other

Loyalty. This word ideally describes "The Doll Lady," her partner Les and the employees, one for all, and all for one. As Ruth Thon, former bookkeeper for the company, so aptly wrote, "The people who worked for them were happy in their work and loyal to their bosses, as well they should be. We were treated as human beings, not machines. As for me, working for them was one of the nicer things in my life and I felt honored to know them."

The employees belonged to the Lady's International Novelty, Handbook and Pocketbook Union. The pay and working conditions were excellent. Though it was strenuous to spend long hours sewing the delicate eye-straining stitching necessary for the small outfits to dress the dolls, Nancy compensated for this by rotating the employees. Those who were involved with sewing had to be rotated to avoid nervous tension caused by the minute fine stitching required for the dolls' costumes. For a short time they would help in various stages of the dolls' preparation.

Another unique example of the feeling toward each other - - employer and employee, was an incident relayed to me by a former secretary of the Nancy Ann Dressed Dolls Company, Corinne Jones. Bear in mind once again that Nancy was shy and loved her home state of California.

When it came time for the American Toy Fair held in New York each year where representatives of various companies displayed their new dolls and toys, Nancy was reluctant to go. She asked Miss Jones to display her dolls for her, along with the company's representatives who at that time were Joseph J. Barnett (East), Leo Scherrer (West), Hugh D. Kenney (Midwest) and Melville Marx (South). Miss Jones was quite young and had never anticipated being sent to New York to set up displays for buyers from all over the world to evaluate and place their orders. She was fearful of flying and had no idea what New York would be like. Nancy lent her her fur coat, which really was a necessity. Miss Jones' New York welcome was a blanket of snow, and since she had not been outside of California up until this time, the cold air was indeed a shock. But even more shocking were the huge crates shipped to New York containing all of the display material that could not be found. The hotel in which the American Toy Fair was held could not locate their crates. She knew they had arrived and was frantic— as there was only one day to get the displays ready. After much pleading, threatening, screaming and crying she knew she would have to take matters into her own hands.

A friend came to help, and late that night they searched the rooms where the manufacturer's dolls and toys were

5

Illustration 5. 6-1/2in. (16.5cm) Hard plastic Nancy Ann Storybook Dolls from *All-Time Hit Parade Series,* shown at the American Toy Fair, New York, in 1948. *Courtesy Corinne Jones.*

Illustration 6. 6-1/2in. (16.5cm) Hard plastic Nancy Ann Storybook Dolls from *Dolls Of The Month Series,* shown at the American Toy Fair, New York, in 1948. *Courtesy Corinne Jones.*

waiting to be set up. After many hours they located their belongings. With a few bribes and some "borrowed" furniture dollies, they began to cart the crates to the display floor. They worked like stevedores and succeeded in transporting it all. Then at the crack of dawn the next day they were able to put it all together. That was a Toy Fair Miss Jones will never forget! But the worst was yet to come, for on the return flight to California, the plane took a deep plunge. It had to land in Chicago in the middle of the night where the phones were all tied up so that she never was able to call home. She has always felt that it had been a "near miss" in the air that night. Nancy and Les were more than pleased with her ability to surmount unforeseen situations and each year thereafter the very best accommodations were made for her.

VOL. II. NO. 47 *Adventures In Business* APRIL 6, 1945

Nancy Ann Abbott

Another example of an employee going way beyond the call of duty is the fashion show presented by Mr. and Mrs. Leo Scherrer in 1955. One day Mr. Scherrer was having lunch with the Bon Marché buyer and discussed the possibility of a Storybook Doll fashion show with him. The idea was for little girls to model costumes, identical to those worn by the Storybook Dolls. The merchandise manager joined them; he thought it was a fabulous idea, and told them to proceed with it and that they would receive all the help they needed. All the doll costumes for the live dolls were made in the Scherrer family room at their home in Seattle, Washington. Donna Scherrer, a niece, was the Master of Ceremonies.

The Scherrers chose girls around 12 to 14 years of age, not over 5 ft. (1.52m) tall and with cute, sort of pudgy legs, so they would really look like dolls. Approximately 300 yards (274.32m) of fabric were used for the 28 costumes. Each of the girls wore three petticoats under her dress, so they really stood out. Each girl was dressed just like the doll she held in her hand. Later taller young ladies also modeled for the Miss Nancy Ann doll creations.

The Scherrers took the show to Denver, Salt lake City and around the Washington-Oregon area between the years 1955—1960. The show was even on television. May Company, Gimbels and Marshall Field and Company were a few of the supporting firms aside from the Bon Marché. The Bon Marché furnished a 12-piece orchestra for each show and gave them a $32,000 order on the strength of the fashion shows. The entire Scherrer family took part in this successful venture. Needless to say Nancy and Les were well pleased.

Many I have been in contact with who had been former employees feel that some of their most treasured possessions are their Nancy Ann dolls. None were willing to part with them. This sentiment perhaps describes more clearly feelings even today regarding "The Doll Lady" more than all the words I may try to use.

The Ups and Downs of "The Doll House"

From the very beginning the struggle to maintain quality and at the same time enable a profit to continue was very difficult in the Nancy Ann Storybook Doll business. As there has always been with all types of businesses, there was a great deal of competition. Many doll manufacturers had started before Nancy; for her business to succeed was doubly challenging as her competitors' names had

Illustration 7. Nancy Ann Abbot appeared on the cover of *Adventures In Business,* April 6, 1945.

already been established.

Nancy and Les worked well together as a team. They were not discouraged easily, if at all. At the end of five years (1937-42), Nancy Ann Dressed Dolls Incorporated had a firm foundation. The company claimed a million dollar gross yearly income. In the 1950s, top production of dolls per day reached 12,000.

The great number of orders requested were not always able to be filled. Fairness to all was practice Nancy followed. Each order was at least partially filled, there was no partiality.

By 1943 there was yet another limited partner, Mr. Frederick E. Anderson.

In 1944 it was necessary to obtain another pottery for the production of bisque dolls. There was a pottery in Stockton, California, that had bankrupt standings; this was added to the company as an investment. This transaction came at a very appropriate time, for the "War Years" had affected many businesses, some being changed over from their former product entirely. The United States Government did not halt their doll production completely in lieu of wartime production goods. They made the dishes for the Navy hospitals. The United States Government reportedly felt the dolls were necessary for the morale standpoint that the Nancy Ann Storybook Dolls provided (many were sent by convoy to Hawaii where soldiers were given a morale boost in buying the dolls and sending

them home to their loved ones). The War order, a contract in the amount of $500,000 for bisque cups, platters and dishes for the Navy hospitals, fit in well with the production of the bisque dolls because the same firing temperature could be used. The dishes did, however, hold down the company's doll production to 4,500 per day, causing yet another shortage in fulfilling requested orders. This experience did give them a forward look for a side-line profit; once the Navy contract was completed, the resulting by-products were plain bisque kitchen bowls. These bowls did not have the Nancy Ann marking. They were sold unmarked to discount houses. The sales helped to replenish money needed to maintain the superior quality of Nancy's dolls and their outstanding outfits.

There were many visiting tours through "The Doll House," mostly children accompanied by adults. The last stop of the tour would be a visit with Nancy Ann, "The Doll Lady" herself, in her office. Her office was unusual for it had an atmosphere more homelike than businesslike. The visitors saw walls of built-in cabinets with sliding glass doors that displayed that particular year's line of doll creations. The comfortable three-piece sectional white sofa added to the visitor's ease. There were no interfering phone calls; Nancy believed calls were too distracting. Those who might need her help, were nearby and could discuss any problems with her in person. (Mr. Rowland handled the outside line of communication.)

Illustration 8. Nancy Ann Abbott with a Girl Scout Troop, visiting her office at 1298 Post Street, San Francisco, California.

The firm was constantly being solicited for donations to this cause and that (this trend will always be). Naturally, they could not honor them all, but if there was ever a cause pertaining to children, Nancy and Mr. Rowland were more than generous. There were many, many donations of dolls and doll cabinets to various children's hospitals and organizations.

The sun seemed to shine brightly for a few years. By the late 1940s Nancy was running the largest doll company in the nation in terms of volume. Then a drastic wild storm of multitude abnormal cell formation took place within part of "The Doll Lady's" body. The diagnosis in February 1956 verified these cells were cancerous. Her attending physicians were skeptical regarding the length of time she had to live. Although she was well aware of all of their prognosis, Nancy's will, courage and fortitude that had sustained her through many a trying time again prevailed during her illness. She continued to be as creative as ever and was determined to spend many hours either sewing a new creation for one of her dolls or for herself.

The 1950s were good years for the company insofar as solidarity. Towards the end of the 1950s Les also became quite ill.

The walls of "The Doll House" started to weaken. Nancy's and Les' health progressively deteriorated. The mounting necessity for additional money made it only practical to sell the site on Post Street. It was purchased by the Standard Oil Company of California. In 1961 "The Doll House" was moved to 424 Ninth Street, San Francisco. The business continued but with great difficulty. There were not as many employees as previously and each that was there struggled to meet requested orders. Nancy, at various times with one arm in a sling, worked for hours on end. She did not know the meaning of "stop." Her grit was immeasurable. Finally Nancy became too weak to stand. From her bed at home she still tried to approve the creations of Fay Redman, whom you may recall had been her right-hand lady almost from the beginning of the company. Mrs. Redman would take what she designed to Nancy's home for guidance and approval. Toward the

end the medical advisers sent word to Mrs. Redman that Nancy could no longer be consulted. When Nancy expired August 10, 1964, her loss was felt by the entire company staff. Their grief continued a lengthy time thereafter. Each day Nancy's absence was felt acutely by all the faithful workers.

Mr. Rowland's health continued downhill, day by day. One cannot but help speculate the drastic affect the loss of a good team partner has on one's health. He realized the company was not going to be able to continue for long under the present circumstances. A sale of the company had been attempted though never consummated. It consequently went into bankruptcy; the turning of the key for the last time was in 1965. A few workers had remained until that time, working without pay.

There is a great deal of understandable sadness with the collapse of "The Doll House," but fortunately all has not vanished.

Though originally planned for children, Nancy's Storybook Dolls became cherished and collectible items. The mothers would purchase the dolls; in many cases I dare say they may have pretended it was to be their child's but once home, that child was only allowed to look at the doll. My sympathy is extended to these former children, who so badly wanted to play with the beautiful, though fragile doll. I and many collectors thank you and your mothers for preserving the dolls in what in many instances appears to be almost absolute perfection, so that one would hardly believe the doll's true age. Hopefully our generation will be able to do the same with existing dolls for the generations to follow.

The popularity of the Nancy Ann Storybook Dolls extended throughout America and into other countries. She received thousands of letters from little ones and adults, and she also answered each one. Nancy did so love children that she found time for their requests and questions in spite of her own busy schedule. I prefer to believe our dear "Doll Lady," Nancy Ann Abbott, and Mr. Allan (Leslie) Rowland, know that we cherish their doll creations and will guard and preserve them for our future generations to admire and enjoy, as we do today.

III.
Original
Advertising

Illustration 10. Bisque dolls, dating from 1942, #250 Princess Minon Minette and #251 Prince Souci from *Powder and Crinoline Series* were used in this Ciro perfume ad.

The need for the usual amount of advertising was not necessary because of Nancy's creative genious with her dolls and their costumes along with Les' outstanding ability to convince others to do the advertising for them.

Many stores had to limit one doll to a customer. When it came to the demand for Nancy Ann Storybook Dolls, it was compared to the line-up of people waiting to buy nylons during the "War Years." Several stores devoted a complete section within their toy department to only the Nancy Ann Storybook Dolls - - the popularity and demand was that great. All seemed to be aware of this "number one doll of its day."

The comic strip "Blondie" by Chick Young even included Nancy's Storybook Dolls within its script.

The Titche-Goettinger Company of Dallas, Texas, used a very appropriate headline in their ads for Nancy Ann Storybook Dolls — "JOYS OF THE PRESENT .... TREASURES OF THE FUTURE." Campbell Soup Com-

pany's advertisement for V-8 Cocktail Vegetable Juices' letter to "Dear Santa" also used the Storybook Dolls' eye-catching appeal for their Holiday ad. Ciro perfumes had Nancy Ann's Princess Minon Minette and Prince Souci in their ads. Greeting Cards by Candid Colored Card Company of New York were so made that the picture of the actual photographs of the Nancy Ann Storybook Doll and the Nancy Ann doll furniture could be detached and framed as miniatures pictures.

Nancy Ann Storybook Dolls received the top award for packaging at the New York Toy Fair in 1940 for the miniature baby girl twins, completely dressed with extra white dresses and knitted shoulderettes. The box was a round pink hatbox with white dots. On top was a large pink ribbon and pink taffeta ruffled pillow on which the twins rested. She also received the Top Buyer Vote Award at the New York Toy Fair in 1942.

Illustration 9. Nancy Ann Storybook dolls even had mention in the comic strip "Blondie."

The following letter of praise was received by Mr. Rowland:

May 6, 1946

Dear Mr. Rowland:

On April 22nd we received your invoice #61371 dated April 16th to the amount of $345.58. This shipment was received on the 26th.

As usual we were delighted beyond words to receive the shipment. When this shipment arrived it was unpacked and instead of telephoning to our customers as we have formerly done we put the shipment in our showcase with signs on the case "Nancy Ann Dolls" "One to a Customer".

We do not handle nylon stockings but our nylons are Nancy Ann Dolls. With no advertising, but by some mysterious grapevine, a steady stream of people came in asking us for Nancy Anns. The enclosed photograph was taken the morning after we received the shipment and we thought it most interesting at the consistent and continued interest and demand for your fine product.

As we have written before, Mr. Rowland, we are 100% Nancy Ann and are not interested in any substitutes or imitations. We do appreciate the fine cooperation we have had from you in these trying times, but are looking forward to the day when we can get enough of a shipment to do some merchandising again and properly publicize these dolls.

Again we want to congratulate you on the fact that your quality has been maintained and that your inspection of each shipment seems to be as rigid as it has ever been. That is another grand reason why we are so enthusiastic over Nancy Ann. Please keep us in mind and if you can get some sizeable shipments to us at an early date, will take off our coats and work for your good company.

Sincerely yours,
Charles Mayer & Company
By *William Huber*

ALZ:gb
A. L. Rowland, Esq.
c/o Nancy Ann Dressed Dolls
1298 Post Street
San Francisco, California

Illustration 11.

Illustration 12. Photograph enclosed with letter shown in *Illustration 11.*

Story Book Doll Set

Illustration 13. This display ad was placed by F.A.O. Schwarz, 745 Fifth Avenue at 58th Street, New York. Original price of this Storybook Doll set was $7.50; it depicts #153 bisque Little Bo Peep (circa 1939).

Illustration 14. Promotional ad placed by Wieboldt Stores, Inc., circa early 1940s.

Illustration 15. These "Great Big Beautiful Dolls" by Nancy Ann were made in limited production during the year 1942. Due to cost they were discontinued.

City of Paris

Now
Great Big
Beautiful Dolls
by
Nancy Ann

Sketched:
Little Rosebud
22 in.   11.95

Made right here in San Francisco by a genius in creating the little stars of Toyland.

Lovely as any of the gorgeous dollies that used to come from France, dressed in rich materials—laces, ribbons and bonnets with flowers. They have actual hair and come in sizes from 18 inches to 22 inches.

Priced from 6.95 to 11.95

Story Book Dolls,
too; over 100
different characters
65c to 2.50

A—Goldy Locks and
the baby bear, $1.00
B—Queen of Hearts.
1.25
C—Pretty maid,
pretty maid, where
have you been. 1.25

Each in an attractive gift box.

Toys, First Floor Annex   *"Chronicle,"   Dec. 8, '42*

WIEBOLDT'S   *Headquarters For*
Storybook Dolls

Perfect for Every Gift Occasion

65c to $1.95

Created by Nancy Ann in 104 different types, the finest selection ever shown . . . and most skillfully made of the finest materials by expert artists. These miniature personalities, 3½ to 7 inches tall, are great favorites among collectors of all ages from six to sixty. Each doll portrays a life-like character familiar to children, in story book fables. The hand-made costumes are actually designed from high quality fabrics, finest printed taffetas, and imported organdies . . . correct hair-styling wigs . . . and made for lots of active use. So keep your youngsters' minds and hands busy . . . make their eyes sparkle . . . with one or more complete series of Story Book Dolls. You'll be delighted to give Story Book Dolls for every gift occasion. Also layaway a series for Christmas giving today!

"Friday's Child"
Days of the Week Dolls
$1.50

"October Maiden"
Months of the Year Dolls
$1.95

The Fable Series
Little Miss Muffet Doll
85c

"Goldilocks"
From the Story Book Series
$1.15

"Southern Belle"
America's Girl Series
$1.35

Interesting, Familiar
Story Book Series Doll
85c

"Queen of Hearts"
Story Book Series Doll
$1.35

"One, Two, Button My Shoe"
Story Book Series Doll
$1.15

"The Scotch Girl"
Around the World Series
$1.35

Hush-A-Bye
Fairy-tale Baby Series
75c

WIEBOLDT'S
106 So. Ashland Blvd., Chicago, Illinois
Please send me the following Story Book Dolls.

QUANTITY	TYPE	PRICE

Name ....
Address ....
City .... State ....
Charge .... Cash ....

More than ever you'll depend upon WIEBOLDT'S friendly prices

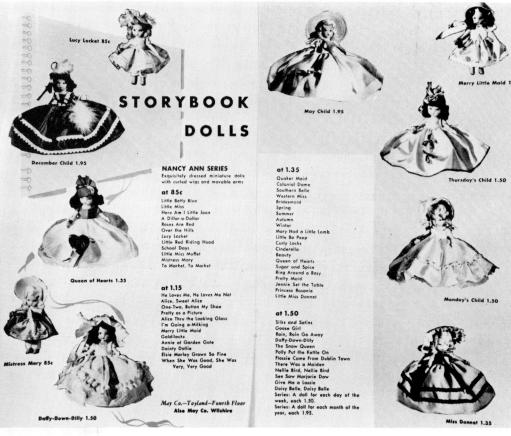

Illustration 17. Right: May Company's 1945 catalog advertisement for Nancy Ann Storybook Dolls showing bisque dolls with movable arms and frozen legs.

Lucy Locket 85c

December Child 1.95

Queen of Hearts 1.35

Mistress Mary 85c

Daffy-Down-Dilly 1.50

STORYBOOK DOLLS

May Child 1.95

Merry Little Maid 1.15

Thursday's Child 1.50

Monday's Child 1.50

Miss Donnet 1.35

NANCY ANN SERIES
Exquisitely dressed miniature dolls
with curled wigs and movable arms

at 85c
Little Betty Blue
Little Miss
Here Am I Little Joan
A Dillar-a-Dollar
Roses Are Red
Over the Hills
Lucy Locket
Little Red Riding Hood
School Days
Little Miss Muffet
Mistress Mary
To Market, To Market

at 1.15
He Loves Me, He Loves Me Not
Alice, Sweet Alice
One-Two, Button My Shoe
Pretty as a Picture
Alice Thru the Looking Glass
I'm Going a-Milking
Merry Little Maid
Goldilocks
Annie at Garden Gate
Dainty Dollie
Elsie Marley Grown So Fine
When She Was Good, She Was
   Very, Very Good

at 1.35
Quaker Maid
Colonial Dame
Southern Belle
Western Miss
Bridesmaid
Spring
Summer
Autumn
Winter
Mary Had a Little Lamb
Little Bo Peep
Curly Locks
Cinderella
Beauty
Queen of Hearts
Sugar and Spice
Ring Around a Rosy
Pretty Maid
Jennie Set the Table
Princess Rosanie
Little Miss Donnet

at 1.50
Silks and Satins
Goose Girl
Rain, Rain Go Away
Daffy-Down-Dilly
The Snow Queen
Polly Put the Kettle On
Flossie Came From Dublin Town
There Was a Maiden
Nellie Bird, Nellie Bird
See Saw Marjorie Daw
Give Me a Lassie
Daisy Belle, Daisy Belle
Series: A doll for each day of the
   week, each 1.50.
Series: A doll for each month of the
   year, each 1.95.

May Co.—Toyland—Fourth Floor
Also May Co. Wilshire

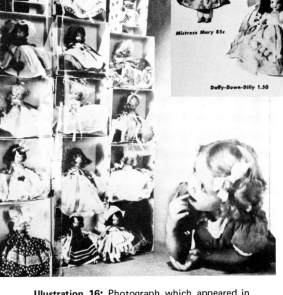

Illustration 16: Photograph which appeared in *Glamour* magazine in 1943. Left to right, top to bottom: #117 School Days (boy); #153 Little Bo Peep; #122 Alice, Sweet Alice; #157 Queen of Hearts; #55 Quaker Maid; #56 Colonial Dame; #90 Spring; #91 Summer; #182 Wednesday's Child is Full of Woe; #159 Ring Around a Rosy, Pocket Full of Posy; #180 Monday's Child is Fair of Face; #155 Cinderella; #183 Thursday's Child Has Far to Go; #161 Jennie Set the Table and #126 I'm Going a-Milking.

Illustration 18. Right: Original advertising from 1947 showing complete sets of Nancy Ann Storybook Dolls with movable arms and frozen legs.

AMERICAN GIRL SERIES... $1.35 each

Order No. D-55—Quaker Maid ★ D-56—Colonial Dame ★ D-57—Southern Belle ★ D-58—Western Miss

SEASONS SERIES... $1.35 each

Order No. D-90—Spring ★ D-91—Summer ★ D-92—Autumn ★ D-93—Winter

DOLLS OF THE DAY SERIES... $1.50 each

Order No. D-180—Monday's Child is Fair of Face
 " " D-181—Tuesday's Child is Full of Grace
 " " D-182—Wednesday's Child is Full of Woe

D-183—Thursday's Child Has Far to Go
D-184—Friday's Child is Loving and Giving
D-185—Saturday's Child Must Work for a Living
D-186—The Child That Was Born on the Sabbath
   Day is Bonny and Blythe and Good and Gay

12

IV. Nancy Ann Storybook Dolls
Bisque Dolls

ABOUT THIS LIST

This list has been compiled from seven of the Nancy Ann Storybook Doll pamphlets which listed the bisque dolls (there are additional such pamphlets but they repeat those previously-mentioned in context). Some names of particular dolls will not be found in this list, such as the 5in. (12.7cm) bisque *Clown (Masquerade Series)* with jointed arms and legs. This is due to the fact that it was made for only a short time before it was discontinued. The baby Quints, sold in a basket and also on a pillow were made in limited numbers, thus they too do not appear in this list. If a particular doll did not sell well or if the cost of production proved too great due to material or hours of labor required, that particular doll's number would be discontinued, or at times, replaced with another doll's name but still retaining the original number. This explains why two different numbers can apply to the same doll.

The numbers Nancy Ann Abbott assigned to each of her bisque dolls do not reflect chronological order; *they were chosen at random.* As can be seen, numbers were skipped. For example the *Flower Girl Series* was assigned numbers 1–6, although the *Around The World Series* was presented *before* and numbered 25–40. These numbers appeared on the doll's circular gold tag (also referred to as the doll's bracelet) and box after 1940; prior to this the numbers could be found on the doll's boxes only.

Each year, almost all outfits were changed in some way. This fact has been known to cause confusion among collectors, particularly if the doll's box with name had vanished, then later the bracelet identification was lost or placed on the incorrect doll. Often the headdress of the dolls did not change from year to year and this sometimes can give clues as to identification. Another factor that Nancy gave consideration to was the various colored wigs offered on many dolls having the same name and number; she felt this would help in identifying certain dolls by their hair color (and little collectors would identify with their own hair color). There were a few dolls whose hair color could not be changed due to the character they represented.

It should be noted that even though *Valentine Sweetheart* was a popular doll and made for several years, it does not appear on any of the bisque doll pamphlets. Also the *Operetta Series* and *All-Time Hit Parade Series* are included in this bisque doll listing since their bodies are bisque (their arms are hard plastic).

It is hoped that these facts have helped to explain why this list is not entirely complete, and why there are **instances of double-numbering.**

Illustrations 19a & 19b. Sample of one of the original pamphlets that came enclosed inside the boxes the dolls were packaged in. This particular pamphlet reflects some of the bisque dolls available.

Storybook Doll Cabinet

Storybook Dolls

Wee Dolls
for
Wee Collectors

'Storybook Dolls'

AMERICAN GIRL SERIES

STYLE NO.	DESCRIPTION
55	Quaker Maid
56	Colonial Dame
57	Southern Belle
58	Western Miss

BRIDAL SERIES

86	Bride
87	Bridesmaid

SEASONS SERIES

90	Spring
91	Summer
92	Autumn
93	Winter

STORYBOOK SERIES
Fairytale—Mother Goose—Fairyland Dolls and Nursery Rhyme

109	Little Betty Blue
110	Little Miss, Sweet Miss
111	Here Am I Little Joan
112	A Dillar-a-Dollar, a Ten o'Clock Scholar
113	Roses Are Red, Violets Are Blue
114	Over the Hills to Grandma's House
115	Lucy Locket
116	Little Red Riding Hood
117	School Days
118	Little Miss Muffet
119	Mistress Mary
120	To Market, To Market
121	He Loves Me, He Loves Me Not
122	Alice, Sweet Alice
123	One-Two, Button My Shoe
124	Pretty As a Picture
125	Alice Thru the Looking Glass
126	I'm Going a-Milking
127	Merry Little Maid
128	Goldilocks
129	Annie at the Garden Gate
130	Dainty Dolly Pink and Blue
131	Elsie Marley Grown So Fine
132	When She Was Good She Was Very, Very Good

STORYBOOK SERIES
Fairytale—Mother Goose—Fairyland Dolls and Nursery Rhyme

STYLE NO.	DESCRIPTION
*133	Little Polly Flinders
*134	Old Mother Hubbard
*135	Jack
*136	Jill
*137	Topsy
*138	Eva
*139	Hansel
*140	Gretel
*141	Gerda
*142	Kay
*143	Mother Goose
152	Mary Had a Little Lamb
153	Little Bo Peep
154	Curly Locks
155	Cinderella
156	Beauty (from Beauty and the Beast)
157	Queen of Hearts
158	Sugar and Spice and Everything Nice
159	Ring Around a Rosy, Pocket Full of Posy
160	Pretty Maid, Where Have You Been?
161	Jennie Set the Table
162	Princess Rosanie
163	Little Miss Donnet, She Wore a Big Bonnet
168	Silks and Satins
169	Goose Girl
170	Rain, Rain Go Away
171	Daffy-Down-Dilly
172	The Snow Queen
173	Polly Put the Kettle On
174	Flossie Came from Dublin Town
175	There Was a Maiden Bright and Gay
176	Nellie Bird, Nellie Bird
177	See-Saw Marjorie Daw
178	Give Me a Lassie as Sweet as She's Fair
179	Daisy Belle, Daisy Belle

UNDRESSED SERIES

1	Hush-A-Bye Baby, 3½ inches
2	Rock-A-Bye Baby, 4½ inches

We do not sell direct

Your local stores can supply additional dolls for your collection

DOLLS OF THE DAY SERIES
Birthday Dolls

STYLE NO.	DESCRIPTION
180	Monday's Child Is Fair of Face
181	Tuesday's Child Is Full of Grace
182	Wednesday's Child Is Full of Woe
183	Thursday's Child Has Far to Go
184	Friday's Child Is Loving and Giving
185	Saturday's Child Must Work for a Living
186	The Child That Was Born on the Sabbath Day Is Bonny and Blythe and Good and Gay

DOLLS OF THE MONTH SERIES

187	A January Merry Maid for New Year
188	A February Fairy Girl for Ice and Snow
189	A Breezy Girl and Arch to Worship Me Through March
190	A Shower Girl for April
191	A Flower Girl for May
192	A Rosebud Girl to Love Me Through the June Days
193	A Very Independent Lady for July
194	A Girl for August When It's Warm
195	September's Girl Is Like a Storm
196	A Sweet October Maiden Rather Shy
197	A November Lass to Cheer
198	For December Just a Dear Oh, I Want a Girl for Each Month of the Year

IN POWDER AND CRINOLINE SERIES

*250	Princess Miñon Minette	
*251	Prince Souci	
*252	Felicia	(Lady in Waiting)
*253	Charmaine	
*254	Delphine	" "
*255	Regina	" "
*256	Theressa	" "
*257	Antoinette	" "
*258	Eugenia Marie	" "
*259	Daralene	" "
*260	Eulalie	" "
*261	Diaphanie	" "

*Temporarily out of stock

NANCY ANN DRESSED DOLLS
SAN FRANCISCO, CALIFORNIA

13

LIST OF BISQUE NANCY ANN STORYBOOK DOLLS
Dolls are 3½in. to 7in. (8.9cm to 17.8cm)

Flower Girl Series

No.	Description
1	Rose
2	Marguerite
3	Daisy
4	Black-eyed Susan
5	Lily
6	Violet

Around The World Series

25	French
26	Swiss
27	Dutch
28	Italian
29	Belgian
30	Spanish
31	Portuguese
32	English Flower Girl
33	Chinese
34	Irish
35	Russian
36	Hungarian
37	Swedish
38	Scotch
39	Mexican
40	Norwegian

American Girl Series

55	Quaker Maid
56	Colonial Dame
57	Southern Belle
58	Western Miss

Masquerade Series

60	Gypsy
61	Pirate
62	Cowboy
63	Ballet Dancer

Sports Series

70	Tennis
71	Sailing
72	Riding
73	Skiing

Family Series

78	Margie Ann in Playsuit (510)
79	Margie Ann in School Dress (500)
80	Margie Ann
81	Margie Ann in Party Dress
82	Margie Ann in Coat and Hat
83	Mammy and Baby
83	Ring Bearer
84	Twin Sisters
85	Brother and Sister (Flower Girl 89 & 87A)
86	Bride, 5-5½in. (12.7-14cm); 268 Bride, 6½in. (16.5cm)
87	Bridesmaid
88	Groom
89	Flower Girl (85 & 87A)
89	Mammy
500	Margie in School Dress (79)
510	Five Little Sisters (78)
2000	Audrey Ann

Seasons Series

90	Spring
91	Summer
92	Autumn
93	Winter

Storybook Series

109	Little Betty Blue
110	Little Miss, Sweet Miss
111	Here Am I Little Joan
112	A Diller-a-Dollar, a Ten O'Clock Scholar (girl)
112	A Diller-a-Dollar, a Ten O'Clock Scholar (boy)
113	Roses Are Red, Violets Are Blue (123)
114	Over the Hills to Grandma's House
115	Little Boy Blue (142)
115	Lucy Locket (124 & 134)
116	Little Red Riding Hood
117	School Days
118	Little Miss Muffet
119	Mistress Mary
119	Alice Thru the Looking Glass (125)
120	To Market, To Market
121	He Loves Me, He Loves Me Not
122	Alice, Sweet Alice
122	Daffy-Down-Dilly Has Come to Town (171)
123	One-Two, Button My Shoe (113)
124	Lucy Locket (115 & 134)
124	Pretty As a Picture (115)
125	Alice Thru the Looking Glass (119)
126	Pussy Cat, Pussy Cat
126	I Have a Little Pet
126	I'm Going a-Milking
127	One-Two-Three-Four
127	Merry Little Maid
127	Richman, Poorman
128	Goldilocks and Baby Bear
128	Goldilocks
129	East Side, West Side
129	Annie at the Garden Gate
130	Dainty Dolly Pink and Blue
131	Elsie Marley Grown So Fine
132	When She Was Good She Was Very, Very Good
133	Little Polly Flinders
134	Old Mother Hubbard (115)
134	Lucy Locket (115 & 124)
135	Jack (175 Jack and Jill)
136	Jill
137	Topsy (176 Topsy and Eva)
138	Eva
139	Hansel (177 Hansel and Gretel)
140	Gretel
141	Gerda (178 Gerda and Kay)
142	Kay
142	Little Boy Blue (115)
143	Mother Goose (145)
144	Snow Queen (172)
144	Polly Put the Kettle On (161 & 173)
145	Mother Goose (143)
146	Old Mother Hubbard (134)

Fairyland or Storybook Series

152	Mary Had a Little Lamb
153	Little Bo Peep
154	Curly Locks
155	Cinderella
156	Beauty (from Beauty and the Beast)
157	Queen of Hearts
158	Sugar and Spice and Everything Nice
159	Ring Around a Rosy, Pocket Full of Posy
160	Pretty Maid
161	Jennie Set the Table
161	Polly Put the Kettle On (144 & 173)
162	Princess Rosanie
163	Little Miss Donnet

Nursery Rhyme Series

168	Silks and Satins
169	Goose Girl
170	Rain, Rain, Go Away
171	Daffy-Down-Dilly Has Come to Town (122)
172	Snow Queen (144)
173	Polly Put the Kettle On (144 & 161)
173	Star Light, Star Bright
174	Flossie Came From Dublin Town
174	Florie Came From Dublin Town
175	There was a Maiden, Bright and Gay
175	Jack and Jill (135 Jack and 136 Jill)
176	Nellie Bird, Nellie Bird
176	Topsy and Eva (137 Topsy and 138 Eva)
177	See-Saw Marjorie Daw
177	Hansel and Gretel (139 & 142)
178	Give Me a Lassie as Sweet as She's Fair
178	Gerda and Kay (141 & 142)
179	Daisy Delle, Daisy Delle
179	The Babes in the Woods

Dolls Of The Day Series

180	Monday's Child Is Fair of Face
181	Tuesday's Child Is Full of Grace
182	Wednesday's Child Is Full of Woe
183	Thursday's Child Has Far to Go
184	Friday's Child Is Loving and Giving
185	Saturday's Child Must Work for a Living
186	The Child That was Born on the Sabbath Day is Bonny and Blythe and Good and Gay

Dolls Of The Month Series

187	A January Merry Maid for New Year
188	A February Fairy Girl for Ice and Snow
189	A Breezy Girl and Arch to Worship Me Through March
190	A Shower Girl for April
191	A Flower Girl for May
192	A Rosebud Girl to Love Me Through the June Days
193	A Very Independent Lady for July
194	A Girl for August When It's Warm
195	September's Girl is Like a Storm
196	A Sweet October Maiden Rather Shy
197	A November Lass to Cheer
198	For December Just a Dear (Oh, I Want a Girl for Each Month of the Year)

Hush-a-Bye Series

200	Short Dress
200	Short Dress and Cape
201	Short Dress and Bonnet
202	Short Dress and Jacket
210	Long Dress
210	Long Dress and Cape
211	Long Dress and Bonnet
212	Long Dress and Jacket
212	Little Miss Lullabye

Little Miss Pattycake Series

230	Short Dress and Bonnet—Organdy Dress
231	Long Dress and Bonnet
232	Short Dress and Crochet Set
233	Short Dress and Rosebud Robe
233	Long Dress and Crochet Set
234	Dress Up Coat and Bonnet
235	Short Dress—Dotted Swiss Coat and Hat
235	Christening— Coat and Bonnet
277	Pillow with Extra Clothes
278	Baby-Basket with Extra Clothes
279	Baby in Bassinette
285	Baby in Rosebud Bassinette
285	Baby in Hatbox with Layette
300	Judy Ann in Story Book with 3 sets of clothes
400	Geraldine Ann from Movieland
2000	Audrey Ann

In Powder and Crinoline Series

250	Princess Minon Minette
251	Prince Souci
	Ladies in Waiting
252	Felicia
253	Charmaine
254	Delphine
255	Regina
256	Theressa
257	Antoinette
258	Eugenia Marie
259	Daralene
260	Eulalie
261	Diaphanie

Operetta Series

301	Orange Blossom
302	Maytime
303	Pink Lady
304	Blossom Time
305	Countess Maritza
306	Irene
307	Naughty Marietta
308	My Maryland
309	Red Mill
310	Rio Rita
311	Floradora
312	Bloomer Girl

All-Time Hit Parade Series

401	A Pretty Girl Is Like a Melody
402	Oh, Suzannah
403	Stardust
404	Beautiful Lady
405	Moonlight and Roses
406	Only a Rose
407	Alice Blue Gown
408	Let Me Call You Sweetheart
409	Over the Rainbow
410	Mary Lou
411	Girl of My Dreams
412	Easter Parade

List of Bisque Nancy Ann Storybook Dolls continued.

Undressed Series

1	Hush-a-Bye-Baby—3½in. (8.9cm)	
2	Rock-a-Bye-Baby—4½in. (11.4cm)	

Additional Items Sold by Nancy Ann Dressed Dolls, Inc.

600	Story Book Box
700	Around The World Box
900	Boudoir Box

Furniture Series   3 Types of Cabinets, Doll Stands

1000	Slipper Chair	1004	Settee
1001	Wing Chair	1005	Armchair
1002	Love Seat	1006	Sofa
1007	Chaise Lounge		
1008	Bed		
1009	Dressing Table, Mirror & Stool		

Illustration 20. Photograph dates from June, 1945, and shows workers for the Nancy Ann Storybook Doll Company in the pottery located in Stockton, California. Here they are working with the clay which is to become storybook characters. There is no question the fine clays from California surpassed the earlier bisque dolls that were made in Japan. The doll bodies both at the Berkeley and Stockton potteries were finished to a smooth perfection by hand-sanding.

Nancy Ann Storybook Dolls produced bisque dolls from 1936 until 1948. By 1943 Nancy Ann Abbott had created 125 different characters, but this number was reduced to 77 when certain materials required to costume different characters were no longer available, or the cost factor proved too great.

At the very start of Nancy's company, dolls' bodies and parts were bought from Japanese suppliers and beautiful materials were imported from Europe; later the company acquired their own potteries which produced the dolls' bodies and parts, and material for the costumes was obtained from across the world. Ill. 20.

The first bisque dolls made by Nancy Ann Storybook Dolls were the *early* Hush-a-Bye Baby dolls (they were also called Rock-a-Bye Baby dolls). They began being made in 1936 and the 3¾in. (9.5cm) dolls are marked on the back: 87 // MADE IN // JAPAN. Reportedly they started to be produced in the United States in 1939 in the 3½ and 4½in. (8.9 and 11.4cm) sizes. A small gold circular sticker was attached to the doll's costume reading either "Nancy Ann Dressed Dolls" or "Judy Ann," later "Storybook Doll" was the marking. The early Hush-a-Bye Baby has painted features, a mouth with a slight opening, hands in a closed fist and cloth booties held on with ribbon. Artists painted the little facial features; hence it is unlikely that there are two exactly alike. The *later* Hush-a-Bye dolls that did not have the open mouths had open hands, giving the appear-

ance of a star. There was yet another Hush-a-Bye Baby produced after this with closed fists. Also, after 1940, they wore a wristband with a gold circular tag giving the doll's number on one side; the reverse side read "Storybook Dolls by Nancy Ann."

It was also Nancy's desire to make collections of "storybook" dolls illustrating nursery tales and jingles. From the latter part of 1936 to 1939 all of the bisque dolls were dressed in original costumes of Nancy's design representing storybook and nursery rhyme characters, costumes from around the world and others. They are marked on the back "MADE//IN//JAPAN//1148," "87// MADE-IN//JAPAN, "JUDY//ANN//USA," or possibly "America." Any bisque doll so marked is usually 5in. (12.7cm) tall with molded hair hidden beneath a mohair wig, molded socks painted a flesh color to match the doll's body and sometimes the left arm is shorter than the right. The shoes are either strapless slippers or boot styles; the only bisque dolls that have shoes differing from this type are some of the babies with booties held on with ribbons.

The socket head dolls were not made until 1940, and these dolls ranged in size from the 6in. (15.2cm) *Groom* to the 6½in. (16.5cm) dolls belonging to *Dolls Of The*

A MINIATURE HAIR-DO

Blue Birds, on an outing sponsored by San Francisco Campfire Girls, watch Alice Ferradin put a wig on a doll in an inspection trip to a doll factory here. The youngsters saw the making of dolls from start to finish. The visit was part of the summer camp program.

LIPS GET PAINTED

"Oh! They're getting their lips painted!" Kay Kaiser whispers to Ann McCook (left) as they watch Lorraine Regan put finishing touches on dolls at San Francisco doll factory. The girls are Blue Birds, "little sisters" of Campfire Girls.

SHE DRESSES A DOLLY

Virginia Smith, 7, wanted to dress a dolly and Mary Reves (at table) let her. The youngsters found thrills aplenty when they visited a San Francisco doll factory on a summer day campers outing sponsored by Campfire Girl leaders for their "little sister" Blue Birds. —Call-Bulletin Photographs.

Illustration 21. Clipping shows some of the steps involved in producing Nancy Ann Storybook Dolls.

Month Series. In 1942 the *In Powder and Crinoline Series* were presented for a short time with the socket head. But then, (with the exception of the Groom), the socket heads were discontinued until the plastic dolls with the painted eyes were produced in 1948. Reportedly in 1943 (though positively in 1944) dolls with frozen legs were produced.

Eventually it became necessary to make a change in regard to the dolls' bodies and parts being imported from Japan--too many parts were broken or had become defective in transport. The "Made in Japan" marking Nancy also wanted changed. From July 6, 1938, on, it is recorded in the United States Patent and Trademark records (July 22, 1941 -- Trademark 389,114) that her dolls were identified with the marking (not necessarily on the doll's body) "STORYBOOK" though other wording was also added such as "STORYBOOK DOLL U.S.A" This marking applies to dolls whether the doll is bisque, plastic with painted eyes or plastic with sleep eyes. It is a fact that the trademark was canceled February 11, 1955.

Bisque dolls which ranged in size from 3½ to 7in. (8.9 to 17.8cm) were offered later. There were a limited number of dolls made with the socket heads and movable arms and legs, as well as dolls with socket heads and frozen legs with movable arms. The frozen-leg-type ranged in size from 6½ to 7in. (16.5 to 17.8cm). One may find bisque dolls dating from around 1947 having a bisque body but with plastic arms, this occurs in the frozen-leg dolls only. This was done to use up material on hand, for the company produced dolls in hard plastic starting in 1948 until 1950. They encountered difficulties with this type of plastic in that the cost factor involved proved to be even greater than the plastic used with the 3½ to 7in. (8.9 to 17.8cm) sleep-eyed versions.

A limited number of bisque dolls had eyes that were painted brown but the majority were painted blue.

As a general rule, there were fewer bisque boy dolls than girls, perhaps reflecting the public's lack of interest in boy dolls at the time. Bisque *Groom* dolls were made in a limited number due to the amount of labor necessary to make their outfits.

The Dionne Quints were also made in bisque in a limited number. They were 4½in. (8.9cm) tall and one set was offered in a basket, the other set on a pillow.

After the Nancy Ann Storybook bisque dolls' bodies and parts were completed at the pottery and sand treated, they were delivered to "The Doll House" for completion. There they were spray-painted a lovely suntan color with a slight sheen and placed on hooks to dry. Shoes were the next step. They were made by placing the doll's feet in a form filled with the desired color of paint. Of course, the form varied in shape, depending upon which type of shoe was called for — either the strapless slipper or boot.

Illustration 22. One of Nancy Ann's first bisque Hush-a-Bye Baby dolls. 3¾in. (9.5cm) tall; marked: "87//MADE/IN//JAPAN;" 1936. Baby has slight open mouth, jointed arms, bent right elbow, jointed legs with bent knees, closed fist and painted features.

The wigs were made of mohair which came from the Orient and Great Britain. They were placed on long poles which lended themselves to easy access when it came to cutting the wig to the desired length (depending upon girl or boy style). The wig was first sewn to a small strip of cloth and glued to the doll's head, secured by a rubber band, then remained in place until the doll was completely dressed with the exception of the headdress. (With no exceptions, all girl bisque dolls from the Storybook Series had something on their head or in their hair. But most of the bisque boy dolls did not have hats; the first bisque Groom doll came without a hat, but later, when made of hard plastic, he appeared with a top hat.) Finally, the doll was dressed, some having little accessories tied to their wrists, along with the circular gold tag with the name and number (after 1940) of the doll on one side; the reverse side read "Storybook Dolls by Nancy Ann." As a last step, the dolls were placed in boxes colored as close as possible to match the doll's outfit whenever possible. The early-type boxes used for the dolls had either pink, blue, red or white

Illustration 24. Each doll is painted bisque. From left to right: 1937; 5in. (12.7cm) **#80** Margie Ann (when dressed); jointed arms and legs, molded painted hair, molded socks painted over the white painted boots; marked on back: "JUDY//ANN//USA." 1939; 5in. (12.7cm) **#60** Gypsy (when dressed); jointed arms and legs, molded hair covered with brown mohair wig, molded socks painted over to match color of body, black painted strapless slippers; marked on back: "STORY//BOOK//DOLL//U.S.A." 1941; 5½in. (14cm) **#80** Margie Ann (when dressed); jointed arms and legs, plain head covered with blond mohair wig, black painted strapless slippers; marked on back: "STORY//BOOK//DOLL//U.S.A." 1943; 5½in. (14cm) **#162** Princess Rosanie (when dressed); frozen legs, movable arms, plain head covered with brown mohair wig; marked on back: "STORYBOOK//DOLL//U.S.A.//PATENT/PEN."

Note: A limited number of dolls only with frozen legs are found marked "NANCY//ANN//STORYBOOK//DOLL//U.S.A." At times a number will also be found under "U.S.A." such as 2-/, 8-/, 10-/, 11-/ or 12-/.

Illustration 23. All dolls are bisque; marked: "STORY//BOOK//DOLL/U.S.A.;" 1941. From left to right: early 3½in. (8.9cm) Hush-a-Bye Baby and 4½in. (11.5cm) Little Miss Pattycake with open hands; 3½in. (8.9cm) Christening Baby and 4½in. (11.5cm) Rock-a-Bye Baby with closed fists.

backgrounds with silver, white or gold dots; the most frequently found later-type boxes had white backgrounds with pink, blue, red or silver dots. There was also a box with white background with a sunburst-type gold circle from which a gold line extended. In 1948, with the start of the hard plastic dolls' production, the boxes came with the words "Nancy Ann Storybook Dolls" printed between the dots; the only exception being the overall Wild West scene used on the Roy Rogers and Dale Evans box (ca. 1955). **Emma Bystrom was an employee of the United Paper Box**

Company of San Francisco and remembers well the detailed instructions that were given for the Nancy Ann Storybook Doll boxes.

The process of using luminous paint on dolls was started in 1941 by Iris Halsey, a registered nurse (she was not an employee of the company). The eyes of Nancy's dolls, as well as portions of their costumes had been selected as those to be used with her harmless luminous paint. That which was so painted, retained a glow for several house after exposure to daylight or strong electric light. In some, their luminous quality can be seen even to this day.

By 1960 the Wonderful World of Disneyland had two exclusive dolls by Nancy Ann. Former Nancy Ann Storybook Dolls employees have stated there were a number of dolls, especially made of plastic, that were made in small quantities for special events or for testing the buyer's market. I have proof of *Alice in Wonderland* and *Cinderella*. These dolls were 10½in. (26.7cm) tall, and their fragile beauty could only be matched by the loveliness of their gowns.

Illustration 26a. Doll marked on back: "MADE//IN//JAPAN//1148." Bisque with movable arms and legs. Illustration shows clearly the knob or bump on head of doll, the molded hair and molded socks that are painted to match doll's body color.

Illustrations 25a & 25b. 5in. (12.7cm) Bisque black doll; molded hair covered with black wig, molded socks painted to match color of doll, black painted high boots; left arm shorter than right arm such as found on early Nancy Ann Storybook Dolls; marked: "87 // Made // Japan." This doll is dressed as #137 Topsy. *Illustration 25b* shows the marking "AMERICA" on the back of a doll, fashioned from a similar mold to that shown in *Illustration 25a* — there is a possibility of this being one of Nancy Ann's molds. **Christy Ackerman Collection.**

Illustration 26b. From left to right: 7in. (17.8cm) bisque socket head; bisque jointed arms and legs; this type of doll is used in the *In Powder and Crinoline Series* in 1942; marked: "STORY/BOOK// DOLL/U.S.A." 6½in. (16.5cm) bisque socket head; bisque jointed arms and frozen legs; this type of doll used in *Dolls Of The Month Series* started in 1941; marked: "STORY//BOOK//DOLL//U.S.A." with either the number "10" or "11" under U.S.A. 7in. (17.8cm) bisque with jointed arms and frozen legs; body type used for dolls in ca. 1944, marked "Storybook Doll U.S.A." NOTE: *Dolls Of The Month Series* were 6in. (15.2cm) and 6½in. (16.5cm).

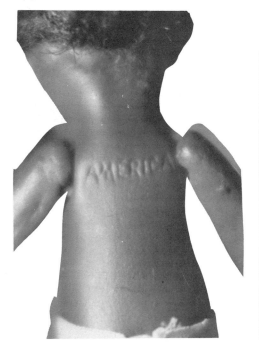

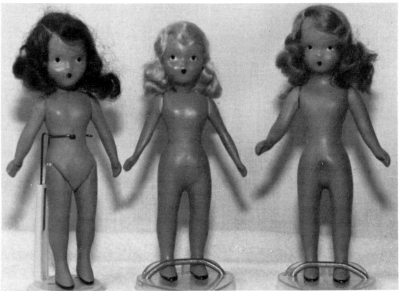

American Girl Series

NOTE: (*The American Girl Series* was discontinued when the plastic dolls were made available.)

Illustration 28. *#55 Quaker Maid*: 5½in. (14cm) Bisque with jointed arms and legs; blond mohair wig; white organdy cap with black ribbon ties. Doll wears a long tan taffeta dress with white organdy material styled in crisscross effect and long white organdy apron. She also wears white pantaloons, white stiff underskirt and black painted strapless slippers. There is a small parcel tied to her right wrist.

Illustration 27. *#55 Quaker Maid*: 5½in. (14cm) Painted bisque with frozen legs; dark mohair wig; white organdy fitted hat with black ribbon ties. Doll wears long gray taffeta dress which has white organdy material styled in crisscross effect over chest and wide white organdy apron. Doll also has white underslip, pantaloons and black painted strapless slippers.

Illustration 29. *#56 Colonial Dame*: 5½in. (14cm) Painted bisque with jointed arms and legs; blond mohair wig; white net cap. Doll has a shocking pink skirt and bodice; there is yellow material over skirt with red and blue flower and leaf print and yellow ribbon trim around bottom of skirt. She also has white pantaloons, white stiff underskirt and black painted strapless slippers. *Marjorie Smith Collection.*

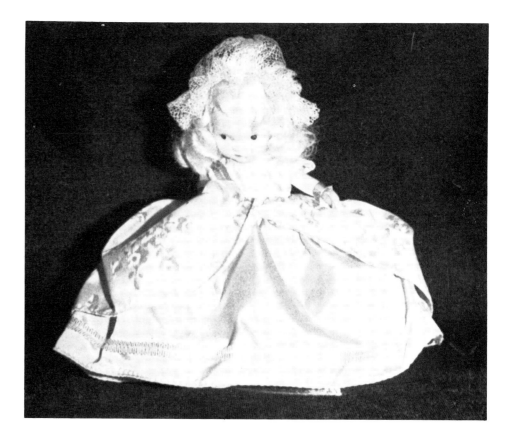

Illustration 30. *#56 Colonial Dame*: 5in. (12.7cm) Painted bisque with jointed arms and legs; dark mohair wig; white net cap with black ribbon as trim.She wears a gray taffeta bodice with white net trim on sleeves and three-quarter length overskirt which is open in center. Her blue cotton skirt has a red flower and green leaf pattern with black ribbon trim around bottom. There is a white underslip, pantaloons with white lace trim and black painted strapless slippers.

Illustration 31. *#56 Colonial Dame:* 5½in. (14cm) Painted bisque with frozen legs; auburn mohair wig; white gathered organdy cap with small white bow on top. Doll's bodice and three quarter length overskirt which is open in center is of blue taffeta. There is white lace trim forming vee on bodice and the skirt is of white cotton with a small flower print and dark blue cord trim around bottom. There is also a white underslip, pantaloons and black painted strapless slippers.

Illustration 32. *#56 Colonial Dame:* 5½in. (14cm) Painted bisque with frozen legs; blond mohair wig; white gathered net cap with small bow on top. Her deep pink taffeta bodice and divided overskirt are worn over skirt of white taffeta with large pink and blue flower print. There is white net trim on the sleeves, white underslip, pantaloons and black painted strapless slippers.

Illustration 33. *#57 Southern Belle:* 5½in. (14cm) Painted bisque with jointed arms and legs; dark mohair wig; large straw hat with black ribbon ties. Her long blue taffeta dress has a small red rose and green leaf print with two rows of black ribbon around bottom. She also wears white underslip, pantaloons and black painted strapless slippers. *Nancy Roeder Collection. Photo by Susan Deats.*

Illustration 34. *#57 Southern Belle:* 5½in. (14cm) Painted bisque with frozen legs; dark mohair wig; large straw hat with green ribbon around top used as ties. Doll wears a long white sheer dress with lavender-green-white flower print in strip formation, one row of green ribbon trim across chest and two rows of green ribbon trim around bottom. She also wears white underslip, pantaloons and black painted strapless slippers.

Illustration 35. *#57 Southern Belle:* 5½in. (14cm) Painted bisque with frozen legs and jointed arms; dark mohair wig; large straw hat with green ribbon around crown, tied under chin. Doll's bodice is white with white cording trim across chest and sleeve edge; her skirt is of nylon-type material with green felt dots and green ribbon trim around bottom. She also wears white underslip with lace trim, white pantaloons and black painted strapless slippers.

Illustration 37. Below. *#58* Western *Miss:* 5in. (12.7cm) Bisque with jointed arms and legs; blond mohair wig; straw hat (flowers missing on right inside rim) with blue ribbon ties. Doll's bodice and lower 2in. (5.1cm) of skirt are of blue cotton with flower print; center is white net. Doll also has white underskirt, molded socks painted to match body and black painted strapless slippers.

Illustration 36. *#58 Western Miss:* 5½in. (14cm) Painted bisque with frozen legs; blond mohair wig; pink and white small check cotton fitted hat with turned back rim and white ribbon ties. Doll wears long pink and white small check cotton dress, organdy apron with white lace trim, white underslip, long pantaloons and black painted strapless slippers.

Illustration 38. *#58 Western Miss:* 5 in. (12.7cm) Jointed bisque with blond mohair wig and black felt hat with black net trim. Doll wears a long taffeta maroon flower print dress accented by two rows of black lace trim around bodice extending to skirt edge. She has a white underslip and black painted strapless slippers.

Illustration 39. *#58 Western Miss:* 5½in. (14cm) Painted bisque with frozen legs; dark mohair wig; white organdy fitted cap with large white net ruffle, large red bow and red ribbon ties. Doll wears plaid taffeta dress (red-blue-white-yellow-green) with red ribbon trim around bottom, white organdy apron with white stitching and small eyelets as trim. She also has white underskirt, long pantaloons and black painted strapless slippers.

23

Around the World Series

NOTE: The *Around The World Series* dolls were started within the first years of the company's existence (late 1930s). They were first marked MADE IN JAPAN//1148; later they were marked STORY//BOOK//DOLL//USA as is the doll shown in *Illustration 40* also found to be marked JUDY//ANN//USA.

Illustration 40. Left. *#25 French:* 5½in (14cm) All-bisque with jointed arms and legs; dark mohair wig with large black satin ribbon tied in huge bow, covering head. Her short dress has a bodice of white organdy with lace trim and skirt of blue polished cotton with one row of light blue ribbon and one row of red ribbon around skirt as trim. The white organdy apron is edged with lace. Wide red felt belt around waist with white stitching forming bow design. Doll has short white panties and black painted strapless slippers. *Jackie Robertson Collection. Photo by Frank Westphal.*

Illustration 41. Below left. *#26 Swiss:* 5½in. (14cm) All-bisque with jointed arms and legs; blond mohair wig; hat of black felt forming a peak. Long yellow organdy skirt is accented by a white bodice with lace trim on sleeves, thin yellow-flowered organdy apron and red felt belt around waist with white stitching. White underslip, short panties and black painted strapless slippers. *Jackie Robertson Collection. Photo by Frank Westphal.*

Illustration 42. Below. *#27 Dutch:* 5½in. (14cm) All-bisque with jointed arms and legs; blond mohair wig; white lace hat. Doll wears long red and white striped skirt, white bodice with sleeves trimmed with lace, long black cotton apron attached at waist and red felt belt around waist with white stitching forming bow design. There is an attached white slip, short underpanties and black painted strapless slippers. *Jackie Robertson Collection. Photo by Frank Westphal.*

Illustration 43. *#28 Italian:* 5in. (12.7cm) Bisque with jointed arms and legs; dark mohair wig; small white organdy headdress with red ribbon tie. Doll has white organdy bodice with puffed sleeves and wide maroon band around waist with white thread stitching forming three bows. The long olive green polished cotton skirt has red-yellow-blue ribbon trim accented with small apron of flower print. Underskirt has blue ribbon trim around bottom. She has short panties and black painted strapless slippers. This doll has molded socks painted over to match coloring of body. Flag is attached to wire slipped through back of outfit. Flags did come with the early dolls that represented countries; this particular doll was made in 1937. Marked "MADE//IN JAPAN // 1148." *Shirley Bertrand Collection.*

Illustration 44. *#28 Italian:* 5½in. (14cm) Bisque with jointed arms and legs; dark mohair wig, small organdy hat with flower print ribbon trim; long cotton dress with white background and small squares of orange, tan and brown of varied designs. Doll has white organdy apron with flowered ribbon trim, white slip and panties and black painted slippers. *Shirley Edgerley Collection.*

Illustration 45. *#29 Belgian:* 5 in. (12.7cm) All-bisque with jointed arms and legs; blond mohair wig; white organdy hat is missing from this doll's picture. Three-quarter length light brown polished cotton dress with white lace trim on each side of bodice. Doll has white organdy apron with lace trim, white underslip, short white panties and black painted strapless slippers.

Illustration 46. *#33 Chinese:* 5in. (12.7cm) Bisque with jointed arms and legs; black hair is painted on; lavender and gray hat with yellow ribbon streamers. Doll wears jacket of gray taffeta trimmed with yellow ribbon, long pants of lavender and gray taffeta with yellow ribbon trim around both legs and black painted strapless slippers. Flag of China attached to wire is slipped in outfit from the back. The doll represents a boy and is marked: "MADE//IN JAPAN//1148;" small circular tag attached to jacket reads "Nancy Ann Dressed Dolls." *Shirley Bertrand Collection.*

Illustration 47. *#31 Portuguese:* 5in (12.7cm) Bisque with jointed arms and legs; dark mohair wig; one-piece cotton hood and cape in gold with circular dot print. Doll has matching apron with black and red ribbon trim, red taffeta bodice, rust taffeta skirt with yellow ribbon trim. There is a white underskirt with yellow ribbon trim, white panties and black painted strapless slippers. Flag of doll's country is slipped through back of outfit. Marked:"MADE IN JAPAN // 1148;"circular gold sticker reads "Nancy Ann Dressed Dolls." *Shirley Bertrand Collection.*

There is another doll dressed as #31 Portuguese (see Illustration 52a), also a 5in. (12.7cm) all bisque with jointed arms and legs; brown mohair wig; light green cloth flower on left side of hair. Her long yellow dress has a red and aqua flower print, white cotton bodice, red felt band around waist and red ribbon trim around skirt. Her aqua felt scarf has wool fringe and she also wears a white underslip, short panties and black painted strapless slippers; from the *Mrs. R.E. Graham Collection.*

Illustration 48. *#33 Chinese:* 5in. (12.7cm) All-bisque with jointed arms and legs; molded painted hair; red ribbon across head with two yellow bows on each side. Doll wears faded blue polished cotton jacket with red ribbon trim along front opening; top and three-quarter length pants are green with red ribbon trim—the remainder of pants' legs are green. This doll has the molded socks painted over to match body color and black painted strapless slippers. Marked "Judy Ann" on back; small round gold sticker on jacket reads "Storybook Dolls." *Christy Ackerman Collection.*

Illustration 49. *#30 Spanish:* 5in. (12.7cm) All-bisque with jointed arms and legs; dark mohair wig over molded hair. Doll wears long dress of red polished cotton with black lace trim around skirt, neck and over shoulders, fashioned into mantilla on head. She has separate white slip, white panties, molded socks painted over to match rest of doll's coloring and black painted strapless slippers. Marked on back "JUDY//ANN//USA." *Jackie Robertson Collection. Photo by Frank Westphal.*

Illustration 50. *#35 Russian:* 5in. (12.7cm) All-bisque with jointed arms and legs; dark mohair wig; red bandanna around head. Doll wears white bodice with blue, red and white trim around sleeves, a three-quarter length multicolored (red-yellow-green-blue-white) cotton skirt with red felt belt around waist. She has a white underslip, short white panties and black painted strapless slippers.

Illustration 51. *#35 Russian:* 5in. (12.7cm) Bisque with jointed arms and legs; glued on auburn mohair wig; red bandanna around head. Her white cotton bodice has white-red-blue trim around sleeves; her skirt has a black background with small flower print (red ribbon trim around skirt) and there is a wide red felt band around waist. Doll also wears short white panties and white painted high-boots.

Illustration 52a. *#31 Portuguese:* 5½in. (14cm) Bisque with jointed arms and legs; brown mohair wig with light green cloth flower on left side of head. She wears a long dress of red, yellow, brown and green print and stripes with a white cotton bodice. There is red ribbon trim around skirt, red felt band around waist and she has an aqua felt scarf with variegated wool fringe. She also wears white underslip, short panties and black painted strapless slippers. *Mrs. R.F. Graham Collection.*

Illustration 52b. *#32 English Flower Girl:* 5½in. (14cm) Bisque with jointed arms and legs; blond mohair wig with pink ribbon with two small felt flowers around hair. She wears a three-quarter length off-white taffeta dress with small flower print and a light pink organdy apron with a gathered organdy ruffle and a band of pink ribbon at waist. A felt flower is tied to her right wrist and she wears pantaloons with small lace trim and black painted slippers.

Illustration 52c. *#34 Irish:* 5½in. (14cm) All-bisque with jointed arms and legs; red mohair wig; gathered white organdy puffed hat. She has a white organdy bodice with black jumper-type top which has white stitching forming bow in center and three-quarter length skirt of gold polished cotton. Doll also has white organdy apron, short white panties and black painted strapless slippers. *Jackie Robertson Collection. Photo by Frank Westphal.*

Illustration 53. *#36 Hungarian:* 5in. (12.7cm) Bisque with jointed arms and legs; dark mohair wig; white organdy flowing headdress around head. Doll wears a white organdy bodice with puff sleeves, black band around waist and long lavender taffeta skirt with yellow ribbon trim around skirt and underskirt. There is eyelet trim across chest and on white organdy apron. She also wears white panties and black painted strapless slippers. Flag of doll's country is slipped through back of outfit. She is marked "MADE //IN //JAPAN //1148;" gold circular sticker reads "Nancy Ann Dressed Dolls." *Shirley Bertrand Collection.*

Illustration 54. *#37 Swedish:* 5½in. (14cm) All-bisque with jointed arms and legs; blond mohair wig; black felt pointed hat. Doll wears a white organdy top with black jumper-type effect, black cotton three-quarter length skirt with one row of yellow ribbon trim and multi-colored apron. Doll also has short white panties and black painted strapless slippers. *Jackie Robertson Collection. Photo by Frank Westphal.*

Illustration 55. *#38 Scotch:* 5in. (12.7cm) All-bisque with jointed arms and legs; blond mohair wig; black angle-type hat with short red ribbon on right side, pulled through to the inside. Doll wears short red and green plaid cotton skirt attached to white bodice and short black jacket. There is a long scarf of red and green plaid that is carried over one arm and under the other arm, giving a sash effect. Doll also has short white panties and white painted high-top boot effect for shoes. *Jackie Robertson Collection. Photo by Frank Westphal.*

Illustration 56. *#38 Scotch:* 5in. (12.7cm) All-bisque with jointed arms and legs; blond mohair wig; black angle-type hat with short red ribbon pulled through to inside. Doll has a short skirt of white, black and red plaid cotton, white bodice, black jacket and scarf of the same material as skirt. She also has short white panties and white painted high-top boot effect shoes.

30

Illustration 57. *#39 Mexican:* 5½in. (14cm) All-bisque with jointed arms and legs; dark mohair wig; straw hat with colors of red, green and tan turned up all the way around. Doll wears long polished cotton dress that has a red and green skirt (lower portion is red) attached to white cotton bodice, accented by multicolored ribbon wrapped around doll's waist, up over shoulders and trailing down skirt in a "sarape" effect. There is a separate white slip, short white panties and black painted strapless slippers. *Jackie Robertson Collection. Photo by Frank Westphal.*

Illustration 58. *#40 Norwegian:* 5½in (14cm) All-bisque jointed arms and legs; blond mohair wig; dark blue felt fitted hat with black ribbon ties. Doll wears a yellow bodice with blue flower print and white organdy sleeves, red polished cotton skirt and white organdy apron with lace trim. She also has a white underslip, short white panties and black painted strapless slippers.

Illustration 59. Above. *#180 Monday's Child Is Fair of Face:* 5½in. (14cm) Bisque with arms jointed at shoulders only; blond mohair wig; blue hat with large flower. Doll wears a gown of peach taffeta with peach organdy overskirt which has two light blue organdy panels down front with nosegays at hem. She also wears white pantaloons and black painted strapless slippers. *Marian Schmuhl Collection.*

Dolls Of The Day Series

Illustration 60.   *#180 Monday's Child Is Fair of Face:* 5½in. (14cm) Painted bisque with frozen legs; blond mohair wig; pink felt hat, turned up rim and trimmed in white lace and blue ribbon. Doll wears a long white taffeta dress with blue and pink flowers and small green leaf print. She also wears a sheer overskirt of dotted swiss-type material trimmed with gathered fabric to match. She has white underslip, pantaloons and black painted strapless slippers. *Nancy Roeder Collection. Photo by Susan Deats.*

Illustration 61. #180 *Monday's Child Is Fair of Face:* 5½in. (14cm) Bisque with frozen legs; blond mohair wig; lace-like hat with pink flowers on right side. Doll's long dress has pink taffeta bodice and underskirt, an overskirt of nylon with two rows of lace trim and pink ribbon on right side of waist. She also wears white pantaloons and black painted strapless slippers.

Illustration 62. #180 *Monday's Child Is Fair of Face:* 5½in. (14cm) Painted bisque with frozen legs; blond mohair wig; blue felt hat with blue organdy bow. She wears a peach taffeta bodice, peach organdy skirt with two panels of blue organdy and two pink cloth flowers at base of each panel, peach cotton underskirt, white pantaloons and black painted strapless slippers.

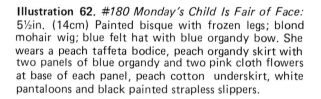

Illustration 63. #181 *Tuesday's Child Is Full of Grace:* 5½in. (14cm) Bisque with jointed arms and legs; blond mohair wig; white lace and narrow blue ribbon with pink rose as headdress. She wears a long light blue taffeta dress with large satin-like flower print and two rows of white lace trim around skirt. She also wears white underslip, white pantaloons and black painted strapless slippers. *Jackie Robertson Collection.*

33

Illustration 64. *#181 Tuesday's Child Is Full of Grace:* 5½in. (14cm) Painted bisque with frozen legs; blond mohair wig; light blue ribbon tied in bow around hair. Her long white sheer dress has large white flower print; her lavender underskirt has light blue ribbon trim. Doll also wears pantaloons and black painted strapless slippers.

Illustration 65. *#181 Tuesday's Child Is Full of Grace:* 5½in. (14cm) Painted bisque with frozen legs; blond mohair wig; blue ribbon around hair along with bow and white cloth flower on right side of hair. Her light blue taffeta bodice is attached to pink taffeta underskirt and overskirt of blue organdy with blue ribbon and wide white lace as trim. She also wears white pantaloons and black painted strapless slippers.

Illustration 66. *#181 Tuesday's Child Is Full of Grace:* 5½in. (14cm) Bisque with frozen legs; light blond mohair wig; light blue ribbon tied in bow around hair. Her lavender taffeta bodice is attached to pink printed taffeta skirt and lavender flocked organdy overskirt. Doll also wears white underskirt, white pantaloons and black painted strapless slippers. *Shirley Nathan Collection. Photo by Howard Nathan.*

Illustration 69. *#182 Wednesday's Child is Full of Woe:* 5½in. (14cm) Painted bisque with frozen legs; auburn mohair wig; blue satin ribbon tied in bow around hair. Her white long taffeta dress has blue cording and white lace as trim. A blue organdy handkerchief with wide, white lace trim is at right side of her waist. Doll also wears white underslip, pantaloons and black painted strapless slippers.

Illustration 67. *#182 Wednesday's Child Is Full of Woe:* 5½in. (14cm) Bisque with jointed arms and legs; red mohair wig; blue narrow ribbon bow with cluster of blue small flowers in hair. Her pale blue taffeta long dress has red and blue small circular dots as design; her overskirt of light blue organdy has handkerchief on right side trimmed in lace. She also has a cluster of flowers tied to wrist, white pantaloons and black painted strapless slippers. (Note: All of the bisque Wednesday's Child dolls have a handkerchief attached to waist of skirt.)

Illustration 68. *#182 Wednesday's Child Is Full of Woe:* 5½in. (14cm) Bisque, dark brown mohair wig; feather in hair. Doll wears printed taffeta dress, with light blue marquisette panel in front and rose colored taffeta slip. There is a marquisette handkerchief on her wrist, and she has a white underskirt, white pantaloons and black painted strapless slippers. *Shirley Nathan Collection. Photo by Howard Nathan.*

Illustration 70. *#183 Thursday's Child Has Far To Go:* 5½in. (14cm) Bisque with frozen legs; blond mohair wig; black felt hat with blue flower and pink ribbon. She wears a long organdy flower print dress, pink ribbon streamers at right side of waist with blue flower attached midway down skirt, white underskirt, pantaloons and black painted strapless slippers.

Illustration 71. *#183 Thursday's Child Has Far To Go:* 5½in. (14cm) Bisque with jointed arms and legs; blond mohair wig; circular blue felt hat with red berries on top trimmed in multicolored looped thread with red bow and ribbon ties. Doll wears a long blue taffeta dress with white small circular design, trimmed in vee on bodice of multicolored looped thread; there is red-green-orange cording around skirt as well. She also wears white underslip, white pantaloons and black painted strapless slippers. *Mrs. R.F. Graham Collection.*

Illustration 72. *#183 Thursday's Child Has Far To Go:* 5½in. (14cm) Painted bisque with frozen legs; auburn mohair wig; small dark blue circular felt hat with green bow on top and ribbon ties. Doll's yellow bodice and front panel is of eyelet material; the remainder of her skirt is dark blue. She also wears a white underslip, pantaloons and black painted strapless slippers.

Illustration 73. *#183 Thursday's Child Has Far To Go:* 5½in. (14cm) Bisque with frozen legs; red mohair wig; felt maroon hat with yellow bow on top. Doll wears a long rose taffeta dress with yellow ribbon trim across chest and around skirt. There is a small yellow bow and flowers near the bottom of skirt and she also wears white pantaloons and black painted strapless slippers.

Illustration 74. *#183 Thursday's Child Has Far To Go:* 5½in. (14cm) Painted bisque with frozen legs; blond mohair wig; dark blue felt hat with small flowers on inside rim of hat and light blue ribbon ties. Her peach taffeta bodice is attached to peach skirt of red and blue flowers and green leaf print. Doll's overskirt is sheer with white embossed flower and stem design. She also wears white pantaloons and black painted strapless slippers.

Illustration 75. *#183 Thursday's Child Has Far To Go:* 5½ in. (14cm) Bisque with jointed arms and legs; golden blond mohair wig; small blue felt circular hat with felt flowers on top and peach ribbon ties. Her long blue taffeta dress has center panel with peach trim on either side. There are also felt flowers on lower right side of skirt. Doll wears white slip and black painted strapless slippers. *Jackie Robertson Collection.*

Illustration 76. *#183 Thursday's Child Has Far To Go:* 5½in. (14cm) Painted bisque with frozen legs; blond mohair wig; large organdy chartreuse bow tied in hair. Doll wears long taffeta maroon dress with white dots and one row of chartreuse organdy around skirt as trim. She also has white underslip, pantaloons and black painted strapless slippers.

Illustration 77. *#184 Friday's Child Is Loving and Giving:* 5in. (12.7cm) Bisque with jointed arms and legs; red mohair wig; blue ribbon tied around hair with large white flower. Doll wears a long dark blue taffeta dress with lace trim across bodice and down, around skirt so as to form a panel effect. There is a parcel tied to her right wrist. She also wears white underslip, pantaloons trimmed with lace and black painted strapless slippers.

Illustration 78. *#184 Friday's Child Is Loving and Giving:* 5in. (12.7cm) Bisque with jointed arms and legs; dark mohair wig; white bow in hair. Doll wears a long white taffeta skirt and bodice with net overskirt of various designs accented by a flower on right side of lower skirt. There is white trim around the edge of the skirt and a parcel is tied to her right wrist. She also wears a white underskirt, white pantaloons and black painted strapless slippers. *Lora Lu Johnson Collection.*

Illustration 79. *#184. Friday's Child Is Loving and Giving:* 5½in. (14cm) Painted bisque with frozen legs; red mohair wig; blue ribbon tied in bow around hair. She wears a peach taffeta bodice and underskirt, and overskirt of peach organdy in white flower print which splits in front to reveal a panel of pink taffeta in pink and blue flower print. There is a row of peach gathered ribbon around skirt as trim and a parcel tied to her right wrist. Doll also wears white pantaloons and black painted strapless slippers.

Illustration 80. *#184 Friday's Child is Loving and Giving:* 5½in. (14cm) Bisque with frozen legs; blond mohair wig; red ribbons tied around hair in bow. She wears a white chiffon dress with tiny dots (red-yellow-blue) and a parcel is tied to her right wrist. She also wears white underslip, white pantaloons and black painted strapless slippers. *Shirley Nathan Collection. Photo by Howard Nathan.*

Illustration 81. *#185 Saturday's Child Must Work For a Living:* 5½in. (14cm) Painted bisque with frozen legs; auburn mohair wig; red ribbon sewn to white rickrack with red bow on right side as headdress. Doll's long cotton dress is small red and white checks accented by black apron. There are two rows of red ribbon trim on apron; one row around skirt. A broom is tied to right wrist with red ribbon. She also wears white underslip, pantaloons and black painted strapless slippers.

Illustration 82. *#185 Saturday's Child Must Work For a Living:* 5½in. (14cm) Bisque with frozen legs; dark mohair wig; stiff white organdy which has been slightly gathered is sewn to trim for headdress, held on with ribbon. Her long white organdy dress has a red broken-line-type flocking design and white organdy apron. There is trim along both sides of bodice, one row around skirt and two on apron. A broom is tied with red ribbon to her wrist. She also wears white underslip, pantaloons and black painted strapless slippers.

Illustration 83. *#185 Saturday's Child Must Work For a Living:* 5½in. (14cm) Bisque with frozen legs; light brown mohair wig; red marquisette hat. Doll wears a red and white printed taffeta dress with red marquisette apron and hat, white pantaloons and black painted strapless slippers. A whisk broom is tied to her right wrist. Her original tag is marked "Story Book Doll USA." *Shirley Nathan Collection. Photo by Howard Nathan.*

Illustration 85. *#186 Sunday's Child (The Child That Was Born on the Sabbath Day is Bonny and Blythe and Good and Gay):* 5½in. (14cm) Painted bisque with frozen legs; blond mohair wig; white felt fitted hat with gathered pink ribbon trim and ties, accented by pink bow on top of hat. Doll wears a long white taffeta dress with gathered pink ribbon to form trim around skirt. She also wears white underslip, pantaloons and black painted strapless slippers.

Illustration 84. *#186 Sunday's Child (The Child That Was Born on the Sabbath Day Is Bonny and Blythe and Good and Gay):* 5in. (12.7cm) Bisque with jointed legs; blond mohair wig over molded hair; white net with gathered pink ribbon to give flower effect with pink ribbon ties for headdress. Doll wears a long, full white net dress with two rows of white lace around skirt as trim and a pink flower made of ribbon on right side of lower skirt. Her satin-like underslip is attached to waist of skirt, and she also wears white pantaloons with lace trim and black painted strapless slippers. *Lora Lu Johnson Collection.*

Illustration 86. *#186 Sunday's Child (The Child That Was Born on the Sabbath Day is Bonny and Blythe and Good and Gay):* 5½in. (14cm) bisque with frozen legs; light blond mohair wig; white felt hat with pink feather. Doll's white taffeta dress is trimmed with gathered pink taffeta, and she also wears white underslip, white pantaloons and black painted strapless slippers. *Shirley Nathan Collection. Photo by Howard Nathan.*

Illustration 87. Below. *#186 Sunday's Child (The Child That Was Born on the Sabbath Day is Bonny and Blythe and Good and Gay):* 5½in. (14cm) Bisque with frozen legs, blond mohair wig; white felt hat with rim turned up on right side to which a flower is attached. Her white organdy dress has one row of white satin ribbon and one row of pink satin ribbon as trim around skirt. There is a white flower on the right side of waist, and she also wears white underslip, pantaloons and black painted strapless slippers. *Jackie Robertson Collection. Photo by Frank Westphal.*

Illustration 88. *#187 A January Merry Maid for New Year:* 6in. (15.2cm) Painted bisque with socket head and frozen legs; dark mohair wig; red taffeta peaked hat with multi-colored ribbon streamers (red-blue-yellow-black-pink). Her black taffeta bodice is attached to red and white taffeta skirt with two rows of black ruffle extending from waist to hemline as trim. She also wears white stiff net underskirt, white pantaloons with white lace trim and black painted strapless slippers.

Illustration 89. *#187 A January Merry Maid for New Year:* 6in. (15.2cm) Painted bisque with socket head and jointed arms and legs; dark mohair wig; red taffeta peaked hat with ribbon streamers (blue-red-pink-white). Doll's long red taffeta dress has white lace trim around sleeves and the center panel of skirt is fabric of multicolored (red-yellow-blue-black-white) horizontal stripes. She also wears white underslip, long pantaloons and black painted strapless slippers. *Nancy Roeder Collection. Photo by Susan Deats.*

Illustration 90. *#188 A February Fairy Girl for Ice and Snow:* 6in. (15.2cm) Bisque with socket head; frozen legs; blond mohair wig; white feather and bow on left side of hair. Doll's long white taffeta dress has flower and scroll flocking design, wide white gathered ribbon to form trim along bottom of skirt and white feather. She also has white underslip, pantaloons trimmed with lace and black painted strapless slippers.

Illustration 91. *#188 A February Fairy Girl for Ice and Snow:* 6½in. (16.5cm) All-bisque with frozen legs; blond mohair wig; white hat with net trim and flowers. Dress is all white with flower on right side of skirt and gathered ruffle as trim. Doll also wears white underslip, white pantaloons pantaloons and black painted strapless slippers. *Shirley Nathan Collection. Photo by Howard Nathan.*

Illustration 92. *#188 A February Fairy Girl for Ice and Snow:* 6½in. (16.5cm) All-bisque with frozen legs; blond mohair wig; white hat with net trim and flowers. Dress is all white with flower on right side of skirt and gathered ruffle as trim. Doll also wears white underslip, white pantaloons and black painted strapless slippers. *Pat Timmons Collection.*

Illustration 93. *#188 A February Fairy Girl for Ice and Snow:* 6½in. (16.5cm) Painted bisque with frozen legs; dark mohair wig; white felt hat with white ribbon ties. Doll wears a long dress in white and pink striped design with white gathered lace and white ribbon streamers at right side of waist. She also wears a white slip, pantaloons and black painted strapless slippers.

Illustration 94. *#189 A Breezy Girl and Arch to Worship Me Through March:* 6½in. (16.5cm) Painted bisque with frozen legs; dark mohair wig; small felt green hat with white feather. Her long green dress has lavender overskirt with cat design. The right side of her skirt is gathered and accented by a light green bow. She also wears white pantaloons and black painted strapless slippers.

Illustration 95. *#189 A Breezy Girl and Arch to Worship Me Through March:* 6½in. (16.5cm) Painted bisque with socket head and frozen legs; blond mohair wig; large black felt hat with turned up rim, white feather, flowers and small yellow bow. Her long taffeta peach dress has white lace trim on sleeves, bodice and down, around skirt to form panel effect. She also wears white underslip, white pantaloons and black painted strapless slippers. *Nancy Roeder Collection. Photo by Susan Deats.*

Illustration 96. *#189 A Breezy Girl and Arch to Worship Me Through March:* 6in. (15.2cm) Bisque with socket head and jointed arms and legs; red mohair wig; dark green flat circular felt hat with red ribbon and cluster of flowers on top. Her long mint green taffeta dress has 2in. (5.1cm) wide white trim and a cluster of flowers on right side. A basket of flowers is tied to her right wrist. She also wears two white stiff underskirts, white pantaloons with lace trim and black painted strapless slippers.

Illustration 97. *#189 A Breezy Girl and Arch to Worship Me Through March:* 6½in. (16.5cm) Painted bisque with frozen legs; blond mohair wig; light pink felt fitted hat with large black bow on top and black ribbon ties. Her black taffeta bodice has two rows of pink cording as trim and her long deep pink, heavy cotton skirt has two rows of black cording as trim. She also wears a white underslip, pantaloons and black painted strapless slippers.

Illustration 98. *#189 A Breezy Girl and Arch to Worship Me Through March:* 6½in. (16.5cm) Bisque with frozen legs and hard plastic arms; blond mohair wig; small flat lavender felt hat with deep pink ribbon and bow on top. Doll wears a lavender taffeta bodice and underskirt, an overskirt of lavender organdy-type material with lace trim around skirt and deep pink ribbon bow attached to right side of lace. She also has white pantaloons and black painted strapless slippers.

Illustration 99. *#190 A Shower Girl for April:* 6in. (15.2cm) Painted bisque with socket head and jointed arms and legs; blond mohair wig; pink ribbon tied in bow around hair. Her white taffeta cape has red-blue-green leaf print, pink ribbon trim and pink ribbon ties. Her long gray taffeta dress has two rows of white trim around skirt. The umbrella matches her cape and is also trimmed in pink. She has a white stiff underskirt, white pantaloons with lace trim and black painted strapless slippers.

Illustration 100. *#190 A Shower Girl for April:* 6½in. (16.5cm) Painted bisque with frozen legs; blond mohair wig; white felt hat with gathered pink ribbon sewn to inside rim and lavender ribbon ties. Doll's long white cotton dress has pink flowers, large and small, with green leaf design giving the appearance of a striped pattern. She also wears white underslip, white pantaloons and black painted strapless slippers. *Nancy Roeder Collection. Photo by Susan Deats.*

Illustration 101. *#190 A Shower Girl for April:* 6½in. (16.5cm) Painted bisque with frozen legs; blond mohair wig; light blue felt hat with flowers on top and peach ribbon tied in bow. Her long peach taffeta dress has blue cording and white lace around skirt as trim and a white lace umbrella with with peach bow is tied to right wrist with white-covered wire. Doll also wears long white underslip, pantaloons and black painted strapless slippers. (Note: Purchased at Carson Perie Scots & Co. for $1.95 in 1947.)

Illustration 102. *#190 A Shower Girl for April:* 6½in. (16.5cm) Painted bisque with frozen legs and hard plastic arms; auburn mohair wig; blue felt open crown hat with white lace and pink ribbon sewn on back. Doll wears a long chiffon-type flower print dress (blue-yellow-red and green leaf) with white lace and narrower blue trim. Her white taffeta umbrella has lace trim and a light blue bow fastens it to right wrist. She also wears white underslip, pantaloons and black painted strapless slippers.

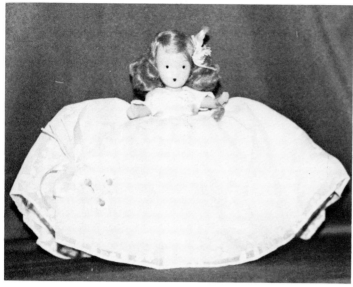

Illustration 103. *#191 A Flower Girl for May:* 6in. (15.2cm) Bisque with frozen legs; dark blond mohair wig; flowers and ribbons in hair. Her light blue taffeta dress has white flocked organdy overskirt with flowers and ribbon. She also wears white underskirt, white pantaloons and black painted strapless slippers. *Shirley Nathan Collection. Photo by Howard Nathan.*

Illustration 105. Above. *#191 A Flower Girl for May:* 6½in. (16.5cm) Bisque with frozen legs and jointed arms; blond mohair wig; blue felt hat with net trim and flowers on left side with pink ribbon ties. Her long pink taffeta dress has a white panel with eyelet at bottom. She also wears a white underslip, white pantaloons and black painted strapless slippers.

Illustration 104. Left. *#191 A Flower Girl for May:* 6½in. (16.5cm) Bisque with frozen legs; blond mohair wig; light blue felt hat with open crown and flowers on right side of hat. Doll wears a blue bodice, an underskirt of taffeta and an overskirt of white net with wide white lace around skirt and flower with pink bow attached to right side of lace trim. She also wears white pantaloons and black painted strapless slippers.

Illustration 106. *#192 A Rosebud Girl to Love Me Through the June Days:* 6¼in. (15.8cm) Bisque with socket head and frozen legs; blond mohair wig; white hair ribbon. Her white satin bodice is attached to printed dimity skirt with white lace, and she also wears white underskirt, white pantaloons and black painted strapless slippers. *Shirley Nathan Collection. Photo by Howard Nathan.*

Illustration 107. *#192 A Rosebud Girl to Love Me Through the June Days.:* 6½in. (16.5cm) Painted bisque with frozen legs; blond mohair wig; white gathered eyelet for headdress accented by rosebud formed with satin and pink ribbon bow. Doll's white sheer long dress has the same rosebud trim across chest, on sleeves and around skirt. In addition, there is 2in. (5.1cm) wide lace trim around skirt as well. She also wears white underslip, pantaloons and black painted strapless slippers.

Illustration 108. *#192. A Rosebud Girl to Love Me Through the June Days:* 6½in. (16.5cm) Bisque with socket head and frozen legs; blond mohair wig; pink ribbon tied in bow around hair. Doll's long organdy dress is white with white flower rose pattern; her taffeta underskirt is light pink with a scattered rose flower pattern. She also has a pink ribbon bow with a cluster of flowers on right side of skirt, white underslip, pantaloons and black painted strapless slippers.

Illustration 109. *#192. A Rosebud Girl to Love Me Through the June Days:* 6½in. (16.5cm) Painted bisque body with frozen legs and hard plastic arms; blond mohair wig; blue felt hat with open crown, pink feather and blue ribbon ties. Doll wears a long yellow taffeta dress in flowered print with blue trim and white lace trim around skirt. She also has a white underslip, white pantaloons and black painted strapless slippers.

Illustration 110. Right. *#193 A Very Independent Lady for July:* 6½in. (16.5cm) Painted bisque with socket head and frozen legs; blond mohair wig; blue ribbon tied around hair in bow. She wears a white taffeta bodice attached to a white dimity skirt with red, white and blue stripes. There is dark blue cording around waist and along bottom of skirt above the white lace trim. She also wears white underslip, pantaloons and black painted strapless slippers.

Illustration 111. Below. *#193 A Very Independent Lady for July:* 6½in. (16.5cm) Painted bisques dressed almost identically in long red taffeta dresses with a panel insert of red and white stripes. There is blue cording as trim on each side of panel and along either side of bodice. Left: Doll has frozen legs; blond mohair wig; dark blue felt hat with open crown and red ribbon on inside rim. There is red ribbon around her waist. Right: Doll has a socket head; dark mohair wig; felt hat with red bow on outside rim. There is a white ribbon around her waist. Both dolls have white slips, pantaloons and black painted strapless slippers.

Illustration 112. *#194 A Girl for August When It's Warm:* 6½in. (16.5cm)
Bisque with frozen legs; dark blond mohair wig; lavender hair ribbon.
Doll's lavender taffeta top is attached to printed taffeta skirt with white
flocked organdy overskirt, and she also wears white underskirt, white
pantaloons and black painted strapless slippers. *Shirley Nathan Collection.*
Photo by Howard Nathan.

Illustration 113. *#194 A Girl for August When It's Warm:*
6½in. (16.5cm) Painted bisque with frozen legs; dark
mohair wig; white felt hat with black bow on top. Doll's
black taffeta bodice is attached to white eyelet skirt with
two black bows. She also wears white underslip, pantaloons and black painted strapless slippers. *Pat Timmons
Collection.*

Illustration 114. *#194 A Girl for August When It's Warm:*
6½in. (16.5cm) Painted bisque with frozen legs and hard
plastic arms; blond mohair wig; blue felt hat with open
crown, pink ribbon sewn to back of felt used as ties and
pink cloth flowers on right side of hat. Her long light blue
taffeta dress has pink cording trim above wide white
lace. She also wears a white underslip, pantaloons and
black painted strapless slippers.

Illustration 115. Left. *#195 September's Girl Is Like a Storm:* 6½in. (16.5cm) Bisque with frozen legs; red mohair wig; rose colored felt hat. Her plaid taffeta dress has white lace as trim and she also wears white underskirt, white pantaloons and black painted strapless slippers. *Shirley Nathan Collection. Photo by Howard Nathan.*

Illustration 116. Right. *#195 September's Girl Is Like a Storm:* 6½in. (16.5cm) Painted bisque with frozen legs; blond mohair wig; burgundy gathered rayon material and blue bow for hat. Doll's dress is light blue; side panels are of 2in. (5.1cm) wide burgundy rayon with blue bows on each side. She also has a white underslip, pantaloons and black painted strapless slippers.

Illustration 117. *#195 September's Girl Is Like a Storm:* 6½in. (16.5cm) Bisque with frozen legs; dark mohair wig; light blue bow and ribbon in hair. Doll wears a long deep pink taffeta dress with lace draped over bodice from shoulder to waist. There is a blue bow at waist, wide lace trim around skirt with narrow blue ribbon above. Doll also wears white underslip, white pantaloons and black painted strapless slippers.

Illustration 118. *#196 A Sweet October Maiden Rather Shy:* 6½in. (16.5cm) Bisque with frozen legs and socket head; red mohair wig; dark maroon felt fitted hat with gathered tan ribbon trim along inside and cluster of flowers on left side. Her long taffeta rust dress has sleeves with caped-top effect, and the panel down the center of skirt is tan. Gathered tan ribbon trim borders each panel. She also wears a long stiff white slip, pantaloons with lace trim and black painted strapless slippers. (NOTE: Another bisque doll with frozen legs is dressed identically to the doll pictured, but it does not have a socket head.)

Illustration 119. *#196 A Sweet October Maiden Rather Shy:* 6½in. (16.5cm) Painted bisque with frozen legs; auburn mohair wig; black peaked hat with yellow ribbon and black lace as trim. Doll wears a dress of long yellow rayon with large bow on right side of waist and two rows of black lace around skirt. She also has a white muslin slip, pantaloons and black strapless slippers. *Shirley Nathan Collection. Photo by Howard Nathan.*

Illustration 120. *# 197 A November Lass to Cheer:* 6½in. (16.5cm) Painted bisque with frozen legs; dark mohair wig; narrow pink and blue ribbons tied around hair in bow. Her dark blue taffeta bodice is attached to sheer white skirt with large blue-red flower and green leaf print. There is gathered dark blue ribbon around skirt as trim. Doll wears heavy white cotton underslip, pantaloons and black painted strapless slippers. (NOTE: *November* doll with bisque head and frozen legs is dressed identically.)

Illustration 121. *#197 A November Lass to Cheer:* 6½in. (16.5cm) Bisque with frozen legs; red mohair wig; open crown felt hat with lace trim and maroon ribbon ties. Doll's long blue taffeta dress has two wide rows of lace trim around skirt. She also wears white underskirt, pantaloons and black painted strapless slippers.

Illustration 122. *#197 A November Lass to Cheer:* 6½in. (16.5cm) Bisque; frozen legs; brown mohair wig; red felt hat with feather. Doll wears red plaid taffeta dress, white underskirt, white pantaloons and black painted strapless slippers. *Shirley Nathan Collection. Photo by Howard Nathan.*

Illustration 123. *#198 For December Just a Dear— Oh, I Want a Girl for Each Month of the Year:* 6½in. (16.5cm) Bisque with frozen legs; brown mohair wig; red felt hat with feather and ribbon. Her red taffeta dress is trimmed with white braid, and there is a feather boa around her shoulders. She also wears white underskirt, white pantaloons and black painted strapless slippers. *Shirley Nathan Collection. Photo by Howard Nathan.*

Illustration 124. *#198 For December Just a Dear— Oh, I Want a Girl for Each Month of the Year :* 6 in. (16.5cm) Bisque with jointed arms and legs and socket head; blond mohair wig; white piece of trim catches tuft of hair along with tiny pink flowers and white ribbon to form headdress. Doll wears a long shocking pink taffeta dress with white lace across bodice and sleeves. There is a gathered effect on each side of dress revealing wide ivory lace which is attached to stiff underskirt. Tiny flowers of light and dark pink with long stems adorn either gathered section, and she also wears white pantaloons with lace trim and black painted strapless slippers. *Jackie Robertson Collection. Photo by Frank Westpahl.* NOTE: This is the doll that is pictured on each pamphlet for the bisque dolls.

Illustration 126. *#198 For December Just a Dear— Oh, I Want a Girl for Each Month of the Year:* 6½in. (16.5cm) Painted bisque with frozen legs; brown mohair wig; dark green ribbon bow in hair. Doll's dark green bodice is attached to long white cotton skirt with white net over-skirt. Green bow and holly adorn each side of skirt. She also wears white pantaloons and black painted strapless slippers.

Illustration 125. *#198 For December Just a Dear— Oh, I Want a Girl for Each Month of the Year:* 6½in. (16.5cm) Bisque with frozen legs and hard plastic arms; mohair wig; red fitted felt hat with white feather and red ribbon ties. Her bodice and underskirt are of red taffeta; her overskirt is of white organdy-type material in a large red flower and green leaf print, gathered up slightly on either side and sewn with red ribbon. She also wears white pantaloons and black painted strapless slippers.

55

Family Series

Illustration 127. *#78 Margie Ann in Playsuit:* 5½in. (14cm) Painted bisque with jointed arms and legs; blond mohair wig; blue and white cotton check sun hat with white ribbon sewn on top of hat and used as ties under chin. Doll's one-piece playsuit is of matching material with vee shaped neckline in back formed by shoulder straps and white trim around pants. She wears black painted strapless shoes. *Jackie Robertson Collection. Photo by Frank Westphal.*

Illustration 128. *#79 Margie Ann in School Dress:* 5½in. (14cm) Bisque with jointed arms and legs; blond mohair wig; blue and white striped cotton hat with turned up rim and white ribbon ties. Doll wears matching dress with white trim around skirt and black painted strapless slippers. *Carole Sladek Collection. Photo by Tod Sladek.*

Illustration 129. Left. *#79 Margie Ann in School Dress:* 5½in. (14cm) Painted bisque with jointed arms and legs; brunette mohair wig; sun-type hat with large rim in front and lavender ribbon which ties under doll's chin. She wears a short cotton dress with white background and small flower print accented by lavender trim around center of skirt. She also has short white panties and black painted strapless slippers. *Jackie Robertson Collection.*

Illustration 130. Right. *#80 Margie Ann:* 5½in. (14cm) Painted bisque with jointed arms and legs; blond mohair wig; blue ribbon around hair tied in bow. Doll wears a short white organdy dress with short panties and black painted strapless slippers. *Jackie Robertson Collection. Photo by Frank Westphal.*

Illustration 131. Upper left. *#81 Margie Ann in Party Dress:* 5½in. (14cm) Painted bisque with jointed arms and legs; blond mohair wig; pink ribbon around hair ties in bow. She wears a short pink taffeta flower print dress with lace trim around sleeves and short white panties. Her legs have the molded socks painted over with white high boots. *Jackie Robertson Collection. Photo by Frank Westphal.*

Illustration 132. Above. *#82 Margie Ann in Coat and Hat:* 5½in. (14cm) Bisque with jointed arms and legs; blond mohair wig. Doll wears a short light blue organdy dress, gathered around neck with small blue ribbon that hangs to hemline, a coat of white taffeta with small pink and blue flowers and small embroidery pattern design and matching fitted hat with "loop" trim and three small flowers on right. There is also "loop" trim on coat and around neckline. She wears short panties with lace trim and white painted high shoes. *Jackie Robertson Collection. Photo by Frank Westphal.*

Illustration 133. Left. *#82 Margie Ann in Coat and Hat:* 5½in. (14cm) Bisque with jointed arms and legs; blond mohair wig; felt maroon hat with red trim turned up at brim. Doll wears a maroon coat with red trim over a short white organdy dress. She also has short white panties and black painted strapless slippers.

Illustration 134 a & b. Below. *#83 Mammy and Baby:* 5in. (12.7cm) Mammy of black bisque with jointed arms and legs; black hair parted in middle. Doll wears long cotton dress of red and white check, long white organdy apron, large white organdy bandanna which is crossed in back, brought over shoulders and tucked into top of apron. Doll also has short white panties and black high topped shoes with white painted dots. The 3½in. (8.9cm) baby is of bisque with jointed arms and legs. Doll has molded hair, bent elbow and closed fist. The white organdy dress has lace trim; the slip also has lace trim. Baby also has cotton diaper and booties with ribbon ties. The gold sticker reads "Storybook Dolls." The early box that was used for Nancy Ann Storybook Dolls is this type— solid color background with small dots. *Shirley Smith Collection.*

Illustration 135. *#85 Brother and Sister:* Both dolls are 5½in. (14cm) painted bisques with jointed arms and legs; dark mohair wigs; black painted strapless slippers. Girl doll has short blue polished cotton dress with raglan sleeves and wide red and white design trim sewn across chest. One pleat extends down center of dress and she also wears white short panties. Boy doll wears costume of matching material — a shirt and short pants. The trim is also the same. *Jackie Robertson Collection. Photo by Frank Westpahl.*

Illustration 137. *#84 Twin Sisters:* 5in. (12.7cm) Bisques with jointed arms and legs and white painted high-top shoes. Left: Blue taffeta dress and hairbow; blond mohair wig. Right: Pink taffeta dress and hairbow; brunette mohair wig. *Carole Sladek Collection. Photo by Tod Sladek.*

Illustration 136. *#84 Twin Sisters:* Both dolls are 5in. (12.7cm) bisques with jointed arms and legs. Left: Blond mohair wig with pink ribbon around hair. Her short dress is of blue sheer-type material with white flower design and pink trim around waist. There are lace cap sleeves and white painted boots. Right: Doll has dark mohair wig, pink dress styled same as doll on left (blue ribbon around hair and blue trim around waist). Also shown is an early box with pink background and small silver dots. *Jackie Robertson Collection. Photo by Rose Mahoney.*

Illustration 138. From left to right, back row: *#87 Bridesmaid* wearing lavender bouquet on wrist with yellow ribbon; *#88 Bridegroom* with socket head in black tuxedo; *#86 Bride* in white satin; *#87 Bridesmaid* dressed in yellow chiffon dress with orange and red flower design. Front row: *#85 Flower Girl* of bisque, 4½in. (11.4cm) with jointed arms and legs. She wears a short pink taffeta dress with lace on sleeve edges and two tiny felt flowers at left side of waist. There is a blue ribbon in her hair and she has white painted high-shoes. *#83 Ring Bearer* of bisque, 4½in. (11.4cm) with jointed arms and legs. He wears a blue taffeta two-piece suit; top opens in front and is trimmed with lace, front and back. A lavender bow ties at mid-chest, holding his top together and he has white painted high shoes. *Jackie Robertson Collection. Photo by Frank Westphal.*

Illustration 139. *#83 Ring Bearer and #85 Flower Girl:* Both dolls are 4½in. (11.4cm) bisques with jointed arms and legs; blond mohair wigs. The Ring Bearer wears blue taffeta long pants, blue vee neck top with white lace as trim and white painted boots. Flower Girl (also named Dee Dee Ann on doll box) wears blue ribbon around hair, short peach taffeta dress with felt flowers on right and white lace trim around sleeves. She also has short white panties with lace trim and white painted boots.

Illustration 140. *#86 Bride:* 5½in. (14cm) Painted bisque with jointed arms and legs; blond mohair wig; white net veil with stiff white crown. Doll wears a long white dress with large satin white flower print, white lace around sleeves, two rows of lace extending from waist to hemline and white satin trim around hemline. There is a white satin ribbon and flowers (lilies of the valley) tied to right wrist. Her white underslip has lace trim as do her pantaloons. She also wears black painted strapless slippers.

Illustration 141. *#86 Bride:* 5½in. (14cm) Painted bisque with frozen legs; dark mohair wig; white veil of netting with white crown. Doll's long white taffeta dress has overskirt of sheer material with flocking design of leaves and stems. There are white flowers and satin ribbon attached to right side of waist. She also wears white underslip, white pantaloons and black painted strapless slippers. *Nancy Roeder Collection. Photo by Susan Deats.*

Illustration 142. *#86 Bride:* 5½in. (14cm) Painted bisque; blond mohair wig; white net veil with white crown. She wears a white taffeta dress with gathered white satin ribbon around skirt, white flowers tied to wrist, white underslip, white pantaloons and black painted strapless slippers. *Shirley Nathan Collection. Photo by Howard Nathan.*

Illustration 143. *#86 Bride:* 5½in. (14cm) Bisque with jointed arms and frozen legs; blond mohair wig; Dutch-type fitted lace cap with white net veil and white bow on left side. She has a white satin bodice, white lace overskirt with white ribbon bow and flowers on left side of waist, white taffeta underskirt and black painted strapless slippers.

Illustration 144. *#87 Bridesmaid:* 5½in. (14cm) Bisque with frozen legs; dark mohair wig; lace and blue ribbon Dutch-type headdress. Her long blue taffeta dress has wide white lace trim around skirt, and there is fern-like trim with light blue ribbon streamers on right side of waist.

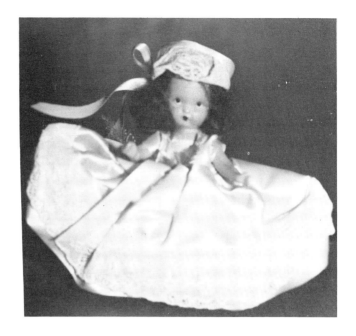

Illustration 145. Below. *#87 Bridesmaid:* 5½in. (14cm) Bisque with jointed arms and frozen legs; blond mohair wig; white lace fitted headdress with open crown and peach bow on left side. She has a peach taffeta bodice and under-skirt; her overskirt is sheer with wide white lace trim around bottom. There is a peach bow and blue flowers on left side of waist and she also wears white pantaloons and black painted strapless slippers.

Illustration 146. Lower left. *#87 Bridesmaid:* 5½in. (14cm) Painted bisque with frozen legs; dark mohair wig; white net hat with open crown, white flowers and yellow ribbon around hair tied in bow. Her yellow taffeta dress has a lighter yellow chiffon-like overskirt with one row of yellow ribbon trim. There are white flowers and yellow ribbon streamers on right side of waist. She also has long white pantaloons and black painted strapless slippers.

Illustration 147. Below. *#87 Bridesmaid:* 5½in. (14cm) Painted bisque with frozen legs; dark mohair wig; Dutch-type hat with open crown and pink satin ribbon is sewn to white lace bow and streamers on right side. Doll has pink taffeta bodice and skirt; overskirt is of light pink organdy with wide white lace trim around bottom. White flowers, pink bow and streamers are at right side of waist. She also wears white pantaloons and black painted strapless slippers.

Illustration 148. *#2000 Audrey Ann:* 5¾in. (14.7cm) Bisque with jointed arms and legs; blond mohair wig; pink bow in hair. Her short lavender organdy dress has wide collar trimmed with white lace and small satin-thread flowers on right side. There is pink ribbon around her waist, and she also wears short white panties and white painted high-top shoes. *Shirley Edgerly Collection.*

Illustration 149. *#510 Five Little Sisters:* 5½in. (14cm) Painted bisque with *brown* eyes; jointed arms and legs; dark mohair wig; light lavender hat with yellow flower print and white ribbon ties. Her one-piece long playsuit is of same material as hat. She has trim around pant legs and white painted high boots. (NOTE: This doll wears an identical outfit to #78 Margie Ann in Playsuit; the fact that the doll pictured here has brown eyes, not blue, differentiates her from blue-eyed #78 Margie Ann in Playsuit.) The doll's box has a white background with dots of gold; center of dot is white and there are small lines of gold around the gold dot. This type of box has been found to be used for #120 To Market To Market, only the back ground color is red. *Ann Blanchard Collection.*

Illustration 150. *#89 Dee Dee Ann Flower Girl:* 4½in. (11.4cm) Bisque with jointed arms and legs; blond mohair wig; blue ribbon tied in bow around hair. She wears a short pink taffeta dress with felt flowers at right side of waist and white lace around sleeves. Doll also has short white panties with white lace trim and white painted boots.

Flower Girl Series

(NOTE: The *Flower Girl Series* were discontinued when the frozen leg bisque dolls were made available.)

Illustration 151. Both dolls are 5in. (12.7cm); all-bisque; jointed arms and legs; blond mohair wigs glued on. These dolls were made in limited number because of lack of popularity. Indicative of early dolls, they both have molded socks painted over to match doll's body color. Left: **#3 Daisy** wears a large white daisy with yellow center and long stem on top of her hair; long white organdy dress with lace trim on sleeves and one row of yellow ribbon around skirt; separate white underslip and short white panties; black painted strapless slippers. *Jackie Robertson Collection.* Right: **#1 Rose** wears a net headdress with pink bow and rose on top, pink taffeta dress with rose on left side of lower skirt; short white panties; black painted strapless slippers. *Carol Westphal Collection. Photo by Frank Westphal.*

Illustration 153. *#5 Lily:* 5in. (12.7cm) Bisque with jointed arms and legs; blond mohair wig; small dark green felt hat with bow on top; green taffeta bodice with white organdy skirt over white taffeta and gathered organdy trim with lily of the valley flowers. *Linda Aringdale Collection.*

Illustration 152. Each doll wears the flower of her name and is 5in. (12.7cm) tall with jointed arms and legs. Proof picture from Marshall Field's Christmas catalog, 1941. Top: **#4 Black-eyed Susan.** Bottom: **#1 Rose; #6 Violet.**

(Also called *Rock-a-Bye Series, Little Miss Pattycake Series* and *Miss Lullaby Series*.)

Illustration 154. These dolls are from approximately circa 1939. At first they were marked "Made in Japan;" later they were marked: STORY//BOOK//DOLL// U.S.A". as the ones pictured here are. This entire set came packaged in the box with names printed beneath each doll (only a very limited number of this set were packaged in this way). Top left to right: **Hush-a-Bye** babies are 3½in. (8.9cm) painted bisques with molded hair and open hands—#200 in short dress; #201 in short dress and bonnet; #202 in short dress and jacket; #210 in long dress; #211 in long dress and bonnet; #212 in long dress and jacket. Next, **Little Miss Pattycake** bisque dolls, 4½in. (11.4cm), with molded hair—#230 in short dress and bonnet; #230 in organdy dress; #232 in crocheted set; #235 in dotted swiss coat and hat; #234 in dress-up coat and bonnet; #233 in rosebud robe and #277 with pillow and layette, this particular doll is 3½in. (8.9cm) tall. *Paula Culbertson Collection.*

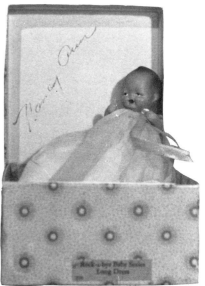

Illustration 155. *#210 Rock-a-bye Baby in Long Dress:* 3¾in. (9.5cm) Bisque; jointed arms and legs; slightly open mouth. Baby wears a long pink organdy dress, white slip, diaper and pink booties tied with pink ribbon. The inside lid was autographed by Nancy Ann in 1938. *Linda Aringdale Collection.*

Illustration 156. Doll from *Hush-a-Bye Series,* ca. 1936. 3¾in. (9.5cm) Bisque with open mouth and molded hair. Baby wears a pink crocheted jacket, long white organdy slip trimmed with lace, white organdy dress and pink booties tied with pink ribbon. The gold sticker reads "Judy Ann." The doll is marked "87//MADE/IN//JAPAN."

Illustration 157. Early doll from *Rock-a-Bye Series;* slightly open mouth indicates this baby was one of the first produced. 3¾in. (9.5cm) bisque doll wears organdy dress with gold sticker which reads "Storybook Dolls." The original box is white with gold dots and lines and is marked Rock-a-Bye Baby Series//Long Dress and Bonnet." Doll marked on back MADE IN//JAPAN; 87 is on top. *Shirley Bell Collection.*

Illustration 158. *#201 Short Dress and Bonnet:* 3½in. (8.9cm) All-bisque baby with jointed arms and legs; open hands; molded hair. Baby wears white organdy bonnet with net gathered for trim and pink ribbon sewed on bonnet and tied under chin. The short white dress is organdy; the white cotton slip has lace trim. Baby also has a white diaper and pink stockinet booties fastened with pink ribbon.

Illustration 160. *#233 Long Dress and Crochet Set:* 4½in. (11.4cm) Bisque with molded hair; painted features, jointed arms and legs. Doll wears long white organdy dress, crocheted bonnet with white trim and crocheted jacket with white trim made of yarn. There is also a white underslip and diaper. *Shirley Edgerley Collection.*

Illustration 159. Left: *#201 Short dress and bonnet:* 3½in. (8.9cm) Bisque with molded hair, arms stretched and fingers open. The dress is short white organdy, gathered at neckline. Doll also wears a cotton-like white diaper, lace-edged slip and matching white organdy bonnet with wide ruffle sewn to brim and tied under chin with blue ribbon. Right: *#200* 3½in. (8.9cm) Bisque with molded hair; jointed arms and legs; and stretched arms and open fingers. Baby wears an organdy dress, white cotton-like diaper, lace-edged slip and white knitted booties tied with pink ribbon. The cape is of pink taffeta with ruffle around neck and pink ribbon ties. *Jackie Robertson Collection. Photo by Frank Westphal.*

Illustrations 161 and 162. *#278 Baby - Basket with Extra Clothes:* Pink basket measures 8in. x 19in. (20.3cm x 48.3cm); blue ribbon is woven along sides and there is a large blue satin ribbon at right upper corner and smaller pink satin ribbons at base and sides. The pink organdy liner is edged with white lace. The baby is a 3½in. (8.9cm) painted bisque. The baby wears an organdy bonnet with pink ribbon ties, a long white organdy dress with one row of white lace extending from neckline to hemline accented by an embroidered rosebud and leaf. The extra clothes consist of a short pink organdy dress, white short slip with white lace trim and pink crocheted jacket. The original box has a blue background with small silver dots.

Illustration 163. *#285 Baby in Hatbox with Layette:* Miniature baby girl twins, 3½in. (8.9cm), completely dressed, lying on a pink ruffled pillow. Extra white dresses and knitted shoulderettes also included. This item won the Packaging Award in 1940 at the New York Toy Fair. Picture obtained from Marshall Field catalog of the time (set originally priced at $3.00).

66

Illustration 164. *#285 Baby in Rosebud Bassinette;* 3½in. (8.9cm) bisque; short organdy dress; organdy slip with lace trim; blue ribbon bow at neck. The bassinet has a cardboard base and cotton lining; there is white satin with small blue flower print for cover. *Carol Westphal Collection. Photo by Frank Westphal.*

Illustration 165. *#300 Judy Ann:* 5in. (12.7cm) Bisque with jointed arms and legs with three extra dresses. She came packaged in a "Storybook."

Illustration 166. *#400 Geraldine Ann from Movieland:* 5in. (12.7cm) Bisque doll with jointed arms and legs and white-painted boots. Complete set included script, eight outfits, spotlights, camera and director's chair. Received the Most Original Toy Contest Award in 1939. Picture obtained from Fred Harvey Gift catalog and originally priced at $5.45.

Illustrations 166a and **b** from *Nelrose Mahoney Collection.*

Illustration 166b.

Illustration 166a.

67

Masquerade Series

(NOTE: The *Masquerade Series* were discontinued by the time the bisque dolls with frozen legs were made available.

Illustration 167. *#60 Gypsy:* 5in. (12.7cm) Painted bisque with jointed arms and legs; molded hair under dark mohair wig; faded blue scarf around head. Doll wears a white organdy top, red sleeveless felt jacket ornamented with small gold-colored discs sewn on each side and stiff yellow organdy skirt with small flower print. Doll also has underskirt of rust polished cotton, short panties, molded socks painted to match dolls' body color and black painted strapless slippers.

Illustration 168. *#61 Pirate:* 5in. (12.7cm) Painted bisque with jointed arms and legs, red mohair wig (for boy doll); red cotton bandanna with small yellow print worn as a headscarf and small black circular felt eye patch attached to black string, held in place under the headscarf. He also wears a large black trifold hat with open crown. Clothing consists of blue and white stripe shirt that is open in front, black short cotton pants, multicolored wide ribbon around waist as sash and black oilcloth around calfs which join black painted high boots for footwear.

Illustration 169. *#60 Gypsy:* 5in. (12.7cm) Bisque with jointed arms and legs; dark mohair wig; red felt fitted hat with yellow ribbon ties. Doll wears a long multicolored cotton dress (blue-yellow-red-green-white) accented by wide taffeta sash, also multicolored and red felt jacket. Doll also wears white underskirt, short panties and black painted strapless slippers. *Jackie Robertson Collection. Photo by Richard Howard.*

Illustration 170. *#62 Cowboy:* 5in. (12.7cm) Painted bisque with jointed arms and legs; short blond mohair wig with molded hair under wig; heavy black felt cowboy hat. Doll wears long black polished cotton trousers beneath light brown chaps with maroon leather-like trim on each side; this same material is used as a belt. Doll's shirt is plaid with long sleeves and collar. There is green ribbon tied around doll's neck as a neckerchief and he has black painted boots. *Jackie Robertson Colelction. Photo by Frank Westphal.*

Illustration 171. *#61 Pirate:* 5in. (12.7cm) Painted bisque with jointed arms and legs; dark mohair short wig (for boy doll); red bandanna worn as a headscarf with yellow flower design and two gold wire long earrings sewn directly to bandanna. His eye patch is of black felt held on by black string. Doll wears short, blue, knitted-fabric pants and yellow long-sleeved knitted shirt accented by multicolored wide ribbon around waist as sash. Footwear is black oil-cloth around calves joining black painted high boots. *Jackie Robertson Collection. Photo by Frank Westpahl.*

Illustration 172. *#63 Ballet Dancer:* 5in. (12.7cm) Painted bisque with jointed arms and legs; blond mohair wig; gathered red net with green sequins as headdress. She wears a red taffeta ballet outfit with two rows of taffeta and four rows of gathered red net. Her bodice has scattered green sequins which are pasted on and she wears black painted strapless slippers. *Jackie Robertson Collection. Photo by Frank Westphal.*

Illustration 173. *#301 Orange Blossom:* 6½in. (16.5cm) Painted bisque with frozen legs and hard plastic arms; blond mohair wig; white satin ribbon around hair with large bow on right side onto which a white veil is sewn beginning at nape of neck. Her long white taffeta dress has white net overskirt with pearl-like flowers and white ribbon streamers. There is wide white lace trim around skirt, and she also wears white pantaloons and black painted strapless slippers.

Illustration 175. *#308 My Maryland:* 6½in. (16.5cm) Bisque with plastic arms; large blue horsehair-type hat styled in two layers with two pink flowers. Her long taffeta large check dress (blue-yellow-green-pink) has 2in. (5.1cm) wide white lace around skirt, topped with pink cording. She also wears white underskirt, white pantaloons and black painted strapless slippers. *Pamela Ann Ford Collection.*

Illustration 174. *#302 Maytime:* 6½in. (16.5cm) Bisque with hard plastic arms. gold mohair wig; horsehair-type large pink hat decorated with tiny blue flowers with yellow centers on stem and wide pink ribbon runs through hat and ties in bow under chin. Doll wears a very pale pink organdy long dress with center insert of embroidered eyelet edged with narrow white lace. There is also lace around lower skirt and a pale pink underskirt is attached to her dress. Tiny blue flowers grace the lower edge of her dress and she also wears pantaloons and black painted strapless slippers. *Jackie Robertson Collection. Photo by Frank Westphal.*

Illustration 176. *#311 Floradora:* 6½in. (16.5cm) Bisque with plastic arms; blond mohair wig two layers of circular horsehair-type pale blue material form hat accented by large flower on right side. Doll's long rayon-type material dress is in small red rose and blue flower pattern trimmed with gathered ribbon and large flower. She also wears a plain pale blue taffeta underskirt, white pantaloons and black painted strapless slippers. *Jackie Robertson Collection. Photo by Frank Westphal.*

Illustration 177. *#310 Rio Rita:* 6½in. (16.5cm) Bisque with frozen legs and hard plastic arms dark mohair wig; black lace mantilla hangs to mid-skirt in back and red flower on green stem is attached to top. Her long bright red taffeta dress has wide black lace around skirt and the same type flower used for mantilla is at left side. There is also an attached stiff cotton slip, white pantaloons and black painted strapless slippers. *Jackie Robertson Collection. Photo by Frank Westphal.*

In Powder And Crinoline Series

Illustration 178. #250 *Princess Minon Minette:* 7in. (17.8cm) Painted bisque with frozen legs; blond mohair wig; gold crown made of paper and aqua feather. Doll's peach taffeta bodice is trimmed with white ruffled lace; her peach taffeta underskirt has 2½in. (6.4cm) wide lace with blue ribbon as trim. Doll also wears a sheer overskirt, white underslip, pantaloons with lace trim and black painted strapless slippers. *Jackie Robertson Collection. Photo by Frank Westphal*

Illustration 179. #251 *Prince Souci:* 7in. (17.8cm) Bisques with jointed legs; dark mohair wigs; both have triangular hats with turned up rims and feather. Left: Doll wears blue hat with ribbon ties, some lace over white bodice and knee-pants of gray taffeta with pink trim. Right: Doll wears blue taffeta coat in small flower print with lace trim on sleeves and on bodice. There is also pink trim around jacket and around knee pants, and there are pink bows on each outer side of pants legs. *Jackie Robertson Collection. Photo by Frank Westphal.*

Illustration 180. *#252 Felica (Lady in Waiting):* 7in. (17.8cm) Bisque with frozen legs; blond mohair wig; light blue ribbon tied in bow around hair. She wears a long light blue organdy dress with insert panel on skirt which is trimmed in lace and has a design of flowers formed by embroidery. Blue cording around apron and skirt complete her dress. She also has a pink taffeta underslip, white pantaloons and black painted strapless slippers. *Jackie Robertson Collection. Photo by Frank Westphal.*

Illustration 181. *#253 Charmaine (Lady in Waiting):* 7in. (17.8cm) Painted bisque with jointed arms and legs; blond mohair wig; two pink bows, one on each side of head. Her pink dress is long with small clusters of white flocking throughout. White braid across chest and on skirt are the trim. She also wears a white slip, pantaloons with trim and black painted strapless slippers.

73

Illustration 182. *#254 Delphine (Lady in Waiting):* 7in. (17.8cm) Bisque with jointed arms and legs; blond mohair wig; pink organdy with white flowers and blue bow for headdress. Doll's long organdy dress is blue and there is pink gathered organdy for the sleeves' edges. A pink and blue satin thread design trim on bodice and shoulders forming a vee in back and there is a white flower and bow on lower right side of dress. She also wears a pink taffeta underskirt, white pantaloons with lace trim and black painted strapless slippers. *Jackie Robertson Collection. Photo by Frank Westphal.*

Illustration 183. *#255 Regina (Lady in Waiting):* 7in. (17.8cm) Bisque with jointed arms and legs; dark mohair wig; wide, white thread-like decoration around head with small pink and lavender flowers. Doll's long light-pink flower print taffeta skirt is attached to plain light pink bodice with white bow design. There is one row of pink and blue trim around skirt. Her long coat is also of pink taffeta in bow design with sleeves edged in gathered white net and narrow pink cording, pink cording also on both sides of coat opening and gathered white net with pink thread along hem edge. (NOTE: This costume is rare for Regina.) *Jackie Robertson Collection . Photo by Frank Westphal.*

Illustration 184. *#255 Regina (Lady in Waiting):* 7in. (17.8cm) Bisque with frozen legs; brunette mohair wig; blue ribbon tied in bow around hair. Her dress of pink taffeta has a pink flocked design, wide lace trim and blue bows. She also wears a white organdy slip with lace trim, white pantaloons with lace trim and black painted strapless shoes. *Carole Sladek Collection. Photo by Tod Sladek.*

Illustration 185. Below. *#256 Theressa (Lady in Waiting):* 7in. (17.8cm) Painted bisque with jointed arms and legs; double bow in center of hair. Doll wears a long white satin dress with large white satin flower design, the overlay is of plain white satin, gathered on both sides. She also wears a white slip and pantaloons with white rickrack trim.

Illustration 186. Above. *#257 Antoinette (Lady in Waiting)* 7in. (17.8cm) Bisque with frozen legs; blond mohair wig, ribbon and bow tied in hair. She wears a long dark blue dress, gathered on right side, accented by a cluster of flowers. She has two underskirts: one attached to dress with wide off-white lace along bottom the other is white with small rickrack trim around bottom. She also wears white pantaloons with rickrack trim and black painted strapless slippers.

Illustration 187. *#257 Antoinette (Lady in Waiting):* 7in. (17.8cm) Bisque with frozen legs; blond mohair wig; ribbon around hair. She wears a long royal blue taffeta dress, gathered up on right side, accented by white bow near waist. There is a stiff underslip sewn to her dress, trimmed with 2¼in. (5.7cm) wide lace. She also wears white pantaloons and black painted strapless slippers. *Jackie Robertson Collection. Photo by Frank Westphal.*

Illustration 188. *#258 Eugenia Marie (Lady in Waiting):* 7in. (17.8cm) Bisque with frozen legs; dark mohair wig; yellow ribbon and bow around head. Doll wears a long yellow organdy-type dress with cap sleeves covered with lace. There is a ribbon around her waist and scalloped lace-like trim around skirt. A yellow bow and flower adorns the lower right side of her dress and she also wears a white underslip with lace trim, white pantaloons and black painted strapless slippers. *Jackie Robertson Collection. Photo by Frank Westphal.*

Illustration 189. *#260 Eulalie (Lady in Waiting):* 7in. (17.8cm) Bisque with frozen legs; blond mohair wig; peach ribbon tied in bow around hair. She wears a long blue small flower print taffeta dress trimmed with gathered peach ribbon along right side of bodice and around skirt. She also has a white underslip, white pantaloons and black painted strapless slippers. *Jackie Robertson Collection. Photo by Frank Westphal.*

Illustration 190. *#259 Daralene (Lady in Waiting):* 7in. (17.8cm) Bisque with frozen legs; blond mohair wig; light lavender bow on left side of hair. Her long dress is light peach with small cluster flower pattern. The lavender overskirt has bows and flowers on each side. She also wears a white slip, white pantaloons with rickrack trim and black painted strapless slippers.

Illustration 191. *#259 Daralene (Lady in Waiting):* 7in. (17.8cm) Bisque with frozen legs; blond mohair wig; lavender ribbon and bow around hair. Doll's long lavender flower print dress has chiffon overskirt and two large bows. She also has a white underslip with lace trim, white pantaloons with lace trim and black painted strapless slippers. *Jackie Robertson Collection. Photo by Frank Westphal.*

Illustration 192. *#261 Diaphanie (Lady in Waiting):* 7in. (17.8cm) Bisque with jointed arms and legs; blond mohair wig; blue hairbow and blue flowers in hair. Doll's dress is a pink sheer with pink flocked flowers and wide lace trim with blue ribbon running through. She also has pink taffeta underskirt, white pantaloons and black painted strapless slippers. *Carole Sladek Collection. Photo by Tod Sladek.*

77

Seasons Series

Illustration 193. *#90 Spring:* 5½in. (14cm) Bisque with frozen legs; blond mohair wig; lavender ribbon around hair and bow at base of neck. Doll wears light green taffeta bodice and underskirt; her overskirt is light green net with white lace trim and lavender flowers and ribbon on right side of skirt. She also wears white pantaloons and black painted strapless slippers.

Illustration 194. *#90 Spring:* 5¼in. (13.3cm) Bisque with dark blond mohair wig; light green ribbon in hair. Doll wears a light green taffeta dress with pink marquisette overskirt accented by flowers. She also wears white underskirt, white pantaloons and black painted strapless slippers. *Shirley Nathan Collection. Photo by Howard Nathan.*

Illustration 195. *#90 Spring:* 5½in. (14cm) Bisque with frozen legs; blond mohair wig; lavender ribbon around hair tied in bow. She has a lavender taffeta bodice, lavender taffeta underskirt and sheer yellow overskirt. She also has lavender bow and flowers on right side of waist, white pantaloons and black painted strapless slippers.

Illustration 196. *#91 Summer:* 5½in. (14cm) Bisque with frozen legs; blond mohair wig; white net hat with open crown and lavender ribbon and bow around hair. Doll wears a light blue taffeta bodice and underskirt; her overskirt is of white organdy with scrolling as a design. There is a cluster of flowers on right side of lower skirt. She also has white pantaloons trimmed with lace and black painted strapless slippers.

Illustration 197. *#91 Summer:* 5½in. (14cm) Bisque with jointed arms and legs; blond mohair wig; light pink felt hat with flowers on right side near back. Her long dress is of light blue nylon-like material with two rows of ribbon around skirt—one pink and one blue. Doll also has pink taffeta underslip, white pantaloons and black painted strapless slippers.

Illustration 198. *#91 Summer:* 5½in. (14cm) Painted bisque with frozen legs; blond mohair wig; pink felt hat with pink satin ribbon ties. Her bodice and lower portion of skirt are pink with small white lines forming squares; from waist to the middle of skirt there is pink netting. 1in. (2.5cm) White lace trims the skirt and she has white underslip, white pantaloons and black painted strapless slippers.

Illustration 199. *#91 Summer:* 5½in. (14cm) Bisque with dark blond mohair wig; light blue ribbon in hair and light blue net picture hat: Doll wears a lavender taffeta dress with printed lavender overskirt, white pantaloons and black painted strapless slippers. *Shirley Nathan Collection. Photo by Howard Nathan.*

Illustration 201. *#92. Autumn:* 5½in. (14cm) Bisque with dark blond mohair wig; flower in hair. Doll wears a light orange colored taffeta dress with pale yellow overskirt with tiny red dot design. She also has white underslip, white pantaloons and black painted strapless slippers. *Shirley Nathan Collection. Photo by Howard Nathan.*

Illustration 200. *#92 Autumn:* 5½in. (14cm) Bisque with frozen legs; red mohair wig; green felt hat with yellow bows on inside left of hat. Doll's bodice is green, her skirt is burgundy accented by the three felt green leaves on right side, connected with yellow ribbon. She also wears a white slip, white pantaloons and black painted strapless slippers.

Illustration 202. *#92 Autumn:* 5½in. (14cm) Bisque with frozen legs; red mohair wig, large flower in hair. Doll has light orange taffeta bodice and underskirt over which there are two layers of overskirt-- the shorter one of yellow organdy; the longer one of light rose organdy. A large orange bow accents costume at right side of waist. She also wears white organdy with check square design and lace trim pantaloons along with black painted strapless slippers.

Illustration 203. *#92 Autumn:* 5½in. (14cm) Bisque with frozen legs; red mohair wig; small red hat with felt flowers, green leaf and yellow ribbon on right side. Doll wears yellow taffeta bodice and long red taffeta skirt with two rows of yellow cord as trim. She also has white pantaloons and black painted strapless slippers. *Jackie Robertson Collection.*

Illustration 204. *#93 Winter:* 5in. (12.7cm) Bisque with jointed arms and legs (pudgy tummy doll); golden blond mohair wig; bonnet of peach velvet lined with peach taffeta accented by small pink flower buds and green leaf attached to outside center of hat as well as light pink ribbon ties. Doll wears long peach velvet dress with long sleeves trimmed in white lace. Also, pink "loop" trim runs down each side of bodice, extending down and around skirt and flower is attached at center. She wears white slip, white pantaloons with lace trim and black painted strapless slippers. *Jackie Robertson Collection. Photo by Frank Westphal.*

Illustration 205. *#93 Winter:* 5½in. (14cm) Bisque with frozen legs and hard plastic arms; red mohair wig; dark green felt hat with large open crown, red bow and two red cherries on right side. Doll wears long green taffeta dress with red trim around waist and two rows around bottom. She also has white underslip, long white pantaloons and black painted strapless slippers.

Illustration 206. *#93 Winter:* 5½in. (14cm) Bisque with frozen legs; dark brown mohair wig; red felt hat. Doll wears a red and white striped taffeta dress and red felt jacket. She also has a white underslip, white pantaloons and black painted strapless slippers. *Shirley Nathan Collection. Photo by Howard Nathan.*

Illustration 207. *#93 Winter:* 5½in. (14cm) Bisque with frozen legs, dark mohair wig; white felt fitted hat with white ribbon ties. Doll wears red taffeta bodice, white felt jacket, white cotton skirt with small red dots and one row red trim around skirt. She also wears white pantaloons and black painted slippers.

Illustration 208. *#93 Winter:* 5in. (12.7cm) Painted bisque with jointed arms and legs; dark mohair wig; red hat of velvet-type material accented by white cord trim with small loops around outside rim and white feather. Her long red dress of velvet-type material has two rows of white cord with small loops as trim. She also wears white underslip, white pantaloons and and black painted strapless slippers. *Nancy Roeder Collection. Photo by Susan Deats.*

Illustration 209. *#93 Winter:* 5½in. (14cm) Bisque with jointed arms and legs; auburn mohair wig; red velvet hat with taffeta inner lining and white feather. Her long velvet dress has red satin bows on each side of skirt, and she also wears white underslip and black painted strapless slippers. *Lora Lu Johnson Collection.*

Sports Series

Illustration 210. *#70 Tennis:* 5in. (12.7cm) Painted bisque with jointed arms and legs; blond mohair wig; white felt sun visor held on with red ribbon. Doll's white two-piece outfit consists of shorts and top made from organdy-type material with red trim up sides of shorts and around neck opening. She also wears white painted strapless slippers. *Jackie Robertson Collection. Photo by Frank Westphal.*

Illustration 211. Below. *#72 Riding:* 5in. (12.7cm) Painted bisque with jointed arms and legs; auburn mohair wig; black felt riding hat with black ribbon ties. There is also black ribbon around waist, white organdy shirt with collar, cotton jodhpurs and black painted boots. *Connie Hart Collection. Photo by Susan Deats.*

Illustration 212. Below right. *#73 Skiing:* 5in. (12.7cm) Bisque with jointed arms and legs; blond mohair wig; dark blue hat with white yarn tassle. Doll wears dark long pants, white cotton sweater, dark blue belt around waist and white painted high boots. *Jackie Robertson Collection. Photo by Richard Howard.*

Storybook Series

(NOTE: Various dolls are also called *Mother Goose Series, Fairytale Series, Fairyland Series* and *Nursery Rhyme Series.*)

Illustration 213. *#109 Little Betty Blue:* 5½in. (14cm) Bisque with frozen legs; red mohair wig; white satin ribbon around hair with bow tied on right side of hair. Her three-quarter length dress is blue dotted swiss with white lace around waist and skirt edge. She also wears long white pantaloons and black painted strapless slippers.

Illustration 214. *#109 Little Betty Blue:* 5½in. (14cm) Bisque with jointed arms and legs; blond mohair wig; large flower on hat. Doll's dark blue dress, felt jacket and hat have red trim. She also wears white pantaloons and black painted strapless slippers. *Pat Timmons Collection.*

Illustration 215. *#109 Little Betty Blue:* 5½in. (14cm) Bisque with frozen legs; blond mohair wig; dark blue felt hat. Doll wears three-quarter length polished cotton blue and white check dress with blue-red-white trim around bottom. She also has long white pantaloons and black painted strapless slippers.

Illustration 216. *#110 Little Miss, Sweet Miss:* 5½in. (14cm) Bisque with jointed arms and legs; blond mohair wig with blue satin ribbon tied in bow around hair. She wears a light blue organdy bodice and short blue skirt with eyelet trim. A blue satin ribbon is around waist and she also wears panties and white high-shoes. *Linda Mortimer Collection.*

Illustration 219. *#111 Here Am I Little Joan:* 5½in. (14cm) Bisque with frozen legs; blond mohair wig; green ribbon tied in bow around hair. Her three-quarter length dress has bodice of green taffeta and skirt with stripes of gray and white. She also wears long white pantaloons and black painted strapless slippers.

Illustration 217. *#110 Little Miss, Sweet Miss:* 5½in. (14cm) Bisque with hard plastic arms; dark mohair wig; light blue open crown felt hat with white ribbon bow. Her three-quarter length cotton dress is pink with a white flower design, and there is blue trim around waist and skirt plus a row of lace trim. She also has white pantaloons and black painted strapless slippers.

Illustration 218. *#110 Little Miss, Sweet Miss:* 5½in. (14cm) Bisque with jointed arms and legs; dark mohair wig; blue ribbon around hair tied in bow. Her short white taffeta dress is in a red and blue dot print with two rows of red and blue trim across chest and around skirt. Doll also wears long white pantaloons and black painted strapless slippers.

Illustration 220. *#111 Here Am I Little Joan:* 5½in. (14cm) Bisque with frozen legs; auburn mohair wig; red felt hat. Doll's dress is a red-green-blue-yellow plaid with red trim around the skirt. She also wears white pantaloons and black painted strapless slipper. *Marjorie Smith Collection.*

Illustration 222. *#111 Here Am I Little Joan:* 5½in. (14cm) Painted bisque with frozen legs; red mohair wig; white felt hat with deep pink ribbon ties. Doll wears three-quarter length organdy white dress with small white broken line pattern and deep pink cording around waist and skirt. She also has white pantaloons and black painted strapless slippers.

Illustration 221. *#111 Here Am I Little Joan:* 5½in. (14cm) Bisque with blond mohair wig; green felt hat with flowers on right. Doll wears light green dress with dark green trim. Doll also wears white pantaloons and black painted strapless slippers. *Marjorie Smith Collection.*

Illustration 223. Right. *#112 A Dillar-a-Dollar, a Ten O'Clock Scholar:* 5in. (12.7cm) Painted bisque with jointed arms and legs; dark mohair wig (cut short for boy). He wears red polished cotton pants, a red and white striped shirt with large white felt collar tied with red ribbon at neck and black painted strapless slippers. *Pat Timmons Collection.*

Illustration 225. Left. *#112 A Dillar-a-Dollar, a Ten O'Clock Scholar:* 5½in. (14cm) Painted bisque with frozen legs; blond mohair wig; blue felt hat with flowers on top and white ribbon ties. Doll's three-quarter length dress is of peach taffeta with gathered peach ribbon around bottom accented by white bow on right side. She also has white pantaloons and black painted strapless slippers. *Nancy Roeder Collection. Photo by Susan Deats.*

Illustration 224. Right. *#112 A Dillar-a-Dollar, a Ten O'Clock Scholar:* 5½in. (14cm) Bisque with frozen legs; blond mohair wig; circular dark green felt hat with red feather and gold ribbon. Doll's dark green taffeta bodice is attached to a long green and white taffeta striped dress with red and green trim. She also wears white pantaloons and black painted strapless slippers. *Jackie Robertson Collection.*

Illustration 226. *#112 A Dillar-a-Dollar, a Ten O'Clock Scholar:* All dolls are 5½in. (14cm) bisques with frozen legs and black painted strapless slippers. From left to right: Girl doll has red mohair wig and yellow ribbon around neck. She wears a green polished cotton three-quarter length skirt, white bodice, black jacket with white felt collar and white pantaloons. Boy doll in middle has a red mohair wig. He wears green polished cotton pants, white shirt and black jacket. Boy doll on right has a dark mohair wig and wears red polished cotton pants, white shirt and black jacket. *Jackie Robertson Collection. Photo by Frank Westphal.*

Illustration 227. Right. *#113 One-Two, Button My Shoe:* 5½in. (14cm) Bisque with brown mohair wig; red felt hat with white flower and green leaves. Doll wears red and white checked shirt, red top, red felt jacket with white trim and black high button shoes with what appears to be three white dots. (NOTE: If there are four white dots on shoes doll is *One-Two-Three-Four #127. Marjorie Smith Collection.*

Illustration 228. Left. *#113 One-Two, Button My Shoe:* 5½in. (14cm) Bisque with hard plastic arms and frozen legs; red mohair wig; white felt hat, turned up at rim with flower on top. Doll wears a large red and white taffeta check dress with wide embroidery-like white trim around skirt and black painted high shoes with three white dots as buttons.

Illustration 229. Above. *#113 Roses Are Red, Violets Are Blue:* 5½in. (14cm) Bisque with jointed arms and legs; blond mohair wig is missing ribbon and flowers. She wears a short white taffeta dress with small rosebud and leaf print, pantaloons and black painted strapless slippers.

Illustration 230. Upper right. *#113 Roses Are Red, Violets Are Blue:* 5½in. (14cm) Bisque with jointed arms and frozen legs; blond mohair wig; large white flower and pink ribbon in hair. Doll has pink taffeta bodice attached to three-quarter length yellow organdy skirt with small flower and green leaf print, pantaloons and black painted strapless slippers. *Jackie Robertson Collection.*

Illustration 231. Right. *#113 Roses Are Red, Violets Are Blue:* 5½in. (14cm) Bisque with jointed arms and legs; dark mohair wig; small black felt hat with lavender flower on top. She wears a three-quarter length dress of dark blue with flower print and two rows of red trim across chest and around skirt, pantaloons and black painted strapless slippers. *Jackie Robertson Collection.*

Illustration 232. *#113 Roses Are Red, Violets Are Blue:* 5½in. (14cm) painted bisque with frozen legs; blond mohair wig; red felt hat with lavender ribbon ties and violets on inner rim. Doll wears three-quarter length red taffeta dress, white pantaloons and black painted strapless slippers.

Illustration 235. *#113 Roses Are Red, Violets Are Blue:* 5½in. (14cm) Bisque with frozen legs; dark mohair wig; blue felt hat. Her long white dress of nylon-like material has a flower print of roses and violets and white scalloped trim. She also has white underslip, white pantaloons and black painted strapless slippers.

Illustration 234. *#114 Over The Hills To Grandma's House:* 5½in. (14cm) Painted bisque with frozen legs; red mohair wig; white felt hat with red ribbon ties. Doll wears a three-quarter length white cotton dress with small red flowers, one row of blue cording and one row of red cording with white thread interwoven as trim around skirt. She also has white pantaloons and black painted strapless slippers. (NOTE: Another costume variation, not pictured, is worn by a doll with jointed legs and red mohair wig. Costume consists of a yellow cotton dress with red dot and blue flower design and red ribbon trim. There is knit smocking on bodice, white lace forms sleeves and her hat is red felt with multicolored trim and red ties.)

Illustration 233 *#114 Over The Hills To Grandma's House:* 5½in. (14cm) Bisque with frozen legs; dark mohair wig; pink felt hat with white trim and pink ribbon ties. She wears a short plaid (blue-green-pink-white) cotton dress with two rows of white trim, white pantaloons and black painted strapless slippers.

Illustration 236. *#115 Lucy Locket:* 5½in. (14cm) Bisque with jointed arms and legs; blond mohair wig; pink ribbon tied in bow around hair. Her dress, almost ankle-length is of white taffeta with small red and blue flowers and leaf print. There is pink ribbon around waist and skirt as trim; matching pink ribbon holds a small gold heart shaped locket around her neck. Doll also wears white pantaloons with lace trim and black painted strapless slippers. *Jackie Robertson Collection. Photo by Frank Westphal.*

Illustration 237. *#115 Lucy Locket:* 5in. (12.7cm) bisque with jointed arms and legs; blond mohair wig. Doll wears three-quarter length white organdy dress with gathered organdy as ruffle around bottom, a half underslip, gold locket around neck, white pantaloons and black painted straples slippers. *Jackie Robertson Collection.*

Illustration 238. Upper right. *#115 Lucy Locket:* 5½in. (14cm) Painted bisque with frozen legs; blond mohair wig; blue felt hat with blue ribbon ties. She wears a three-quarter length blue taffeta dress in darker blue flower print design accented by one row of white lace across chest and around hemline. She also has white pantaloons and black painted strapless slippers.

Illustration 239. *#115 Lucy Locket:* 5½in. (14cm) Bisque with frozen legs; red mohair wig; dark lavender felt bonnet with ribbon ties. Her three-quarter length lavender dress has white lace trim and there is wide ribbon around shoulders of doll, crossed in front to facilitate dolls for shipment. She also wears white pantaloons and black painted strapless slippers. *Clara McCann Collection.*

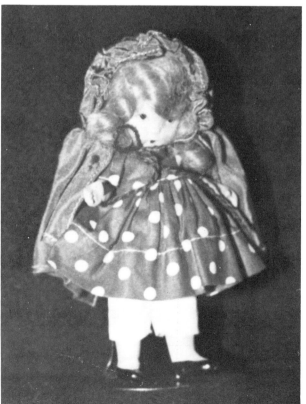

Illustration 240. Above. *#115 Little Boy Blue:* (Left) Painted bisque with frozen legs; blond mohair wig. He is dressed in a two piece light blue taffeta suit with lace trim around collar and sleeves. He also has black painted strapless slippers. (Right) Painted bisque with frozen legs. This doll is dressed in light blue taffeta trousers, an orange taffeta shirt and royal blue felt jacket. There is an orange ribbon tied in bow under chin and black painted strapless slippers are his footwear. *Jackie Robertson Collection. Photo by Frank Westphal.*

Illustration 241. *#116 Little Red Riding Hood:* 5in. (12.7cm) Bisque with jointed arms and legs; blond mohair wig. Doll's dress is of polished cotton - red with a large white dot pattern. The hood and cape as one-piece and of red taffeta, gathered with red cording through hood and tied under chin. She also wears white pantaloons and black painted strapless slippers.

Illustration 242. *#116 Little Red Riding Hood:* The three dolls are 5½in. (14cm) Painted bisques with frozen legs, and have black painted strapless slippers. From left to right: Blond mohair wig; red taffeta hood and cape, white organdy dress; short white panties. Dark mohair wig; red felt hood with peak attached to cape; cotton plaid dress (red-white-green-black); white pantaloons. Dark mohair wig; red taffeta hood and cape; white organdy dress and short white panties.

Illustration 243. Left. *#117 School Days:* 5½in. (14cm) Bisque with frozen legs and jointed arms; short auburn mohair wig. Boy doll wears shirt of large red and white check pattern, red polished cotton pants, dark blue felt jacket and black painted strapless slippers. *Jackie Robertson Collection.*

Illustration 244. Right. *#117 School Days:* 5in. (12.7cm) Painted bisque with jointed arms and legs; blond mohair wig; white ribbon tied in bow around hair. She wears a short cotton red and white small check dress with white trim with loops across chest and around skirt. She also has short white panties and white painted high-boots.

Illustration 245. Left. # *117 School Days:* 5½in. (14cm) Painted bisque with frozen legs; dark mohair wig; white ribbon tied in bow around hair. She wears a short lavender cotton dress; front of bodice and apron are of small red and white checked material. There is white trim across bottom of apron. She also wears white pantaloons and black painted strapless slippers.

Illustration 246. Below. *#117 School Days:* 5½in. (14cm) Bisque with jointed arms and frozen legs; dark mohair wig; pink fitted felt hat with pink ribbon ties. Her three-quarter length white cotton dress has small flowers and dots as print; there is pink cording around waist and skirt as trim. She also wears white pantaloons with lace trim and black painted strapless slippers. *Jackie Robertson Collection.*

Illustration 247. Lower left. *#117 School Days:* Bisque with red mohair wig; dark blue ribbon around hair. Doll's dress is of white organdy with small blue dot print and dark blue trim around waist and lower skirt. She also wears white pantaloons and black painted strapless slippers. *Shirley Bell Collection.*

Illustration 248. Below. *#117 School Days:* 5½in. (14cm) Bisque with frozen legs; blond mohair wig; white ribbon around hair. Her bodice and apron are of pink taffeta accented by blue and white trim; her three-quarter length skirt is of blue and white checked cotton seersucker. She also wears white pantaloons and black painted strapless slippers.

Illustration 249. Above *#117 School Days:* 5½in. (14cm) Bisque with jointed arms and frozen legs; blond mohair wig; blue ribbon tied in bow around hair. Her three-quarter length dark blue dress has a bodice and apron in blue and white check. Her apron has two rows of white trim. She also wears white pantaloons and black painted strapless slippers. *Jackie Robertson Collection.*

Illustration 250. *#118 Little Miss Muffet:* 5in. (12.7cm) Bisque with jointed arms and legs; auburn mohair wig; yellow organdy puffed hat. Doll's three-quarter length taffeta dress with small flower print is accented by yellow organdy apron. There is red trim around waist and on the apron. She also wears white underslip, white pantaloons and black painted strapless slippers.

Illustration 251. Lower left. *#118 Little Miss Muffet:* 5½in. (14cm) Bisque with jointed arms and legs; dark mohair wig; blue felt hat with ribbon ties. Doll wears three-quarter length white organdy dress with green leaf and yellow and blue flower print, white organdy apron with gathered ruffle at bottom, white pantaloons and black painted strapless slippers. *Jackie Robertson Collection.*

Illustration 252. *#118 Little Miss Muffet:* 5½in. (14cm) Painted bisque with frozen legs; blond mohair wig; white organdy headdress with lavender ribbon ties. Doll wears three-quarter length dress white with large green leaf and flower print, a white organdy apron with gathered white organdy ruffle on bottom, white pantaloons and black painted strapless slippers. *Nancy Roeder Collection. Photo by Susan Deats.*

Illustration 253. Above. *#119 Mistress Mary:* 5½in. (14cm) Painted bisque with frozen legs; blond mohair wig; white felt hat with pink cloth flowers in center of inside rim and pink ribbon ties. She wears a three-quarter length cotton print dress (white flowers with blue bows), white pantaloons and black painted strapless slippers.

Illustration 254. Upper right. *#119 Mistress Mary:* 5½in. (14cm) Bisque with jointed arms and legs; blond mohair wig; white felt hat with flower on inside rim and white ribbon tied in bow around hair. Doll wears a blue cotton flower print three-quarter length dress with white trim around waist, white pantaloons and black painted strapless slippers. *Jackie Robertson Collection.*

Illustration 255. Lower right. *#119 Mistress Mary:* 5½in. (14cm) Bisque with blond mohair wig; pink felt hat. Doll wears short lavender taffeta dress, printed taffeta apron, white underskirt, white pantaloons and black painted strapless slippers. *Shirley Nathan Collection. Photo by Howard Nathan.*

Illustration 256. *#120 To Market, To Market:* 5in. (12.7cm) Painted bisque with jointed arms and legs; dark mohair wig; red felt hat with red ribbon ties. Her short dress has bodice and apron of white cotton with flower print (blue-yellow-red) and skirt of white organdy. She also wears a short white underslip, white pantaloons and black painted strapless slippers. This doll has the molded socks painted to match color of doll's body. The box is of a rare design with red background and gold circles. *Connie Hart Collection. Photo by Susan Deats.*

Illustration 258. *#120 To Market, To Market:* 5½in. (14cm) Bisque with frozen legs; dark mohair wig; dark blue fitted felt hat with red ribbon ties. Doll wears three-quarter length dress which has a bodice of dark blue taffeta and skirt of red and white cotton crepe. She also wears white pantaloons and black painted strapless slippers.

Illustration 257. *#120 To Market, To Market:* 5½in. (14cm) Bisque with frozen legs; dark mohair wig; red felt hat with red ribbon ties. She wears a short cotton dress in a small tan and white check with two rows of red trim around lower skirt. She also wears white pantaloons and black painted strapless slippers.

Illustration 259. *#120 To Market, To Market:* 5½in. (14cm) Bisque with jointed arms and frozen legs; dark mohair wig; blue felt hat with burgundy bow on top and red ribbon ties. Doll wears three-quarter length burgundy taffeta dress with blue ribbon around waist and skirt as trim, white pantaloons and black painted strapless slippers. *Jackie Robertson Collection.*

Illustration 260. *#120 To Market, To Market:* 5½in. (14cm) Bisque with frozen legs; dark blond mohair wit; maroon fitted felt hat with yellow trim along rim of hat and red ribbon ties. Her bodice, with yellow trim, and apron are both red; her skirt is yellow taffeta with red dots. She also wears white pantaloons and black painted strapless slippers. *Ginny Zeidler Collection.*

Illustration 261. *#121 He Loves Me, He Loves Me Not:* 5½in. (14cm) Painted bisque with frozen legs; blond mohair wig; maroon felt hat with white daisy on right side. Doll wears a three-quarter length pink dress with white lace across chest and around skirt. She has white pantaloons and black painted strapless slippers.

Illustration 262. *#121 He Loves Me, He Loves Me Not:* 5½in. (14cm) Painted bisque with frozen legs; dark mohair wig; lavender ribbon around hair ties in bow. Her short lavender taffeta dress has white trim over shoulders, across chest and around skirt. There is a lavender bow with daisy attached to the right side of skirt's white trim. She also wears white pantaloons and black painted strapless slippers. *Nancy Roeder Collection. Photo by Susan Deats.*

Illustration 263. *#121 He Loves Me, He Loves Me Not:* 5½in. (14cm) Bisque with jointed arms and frozen legs; auburn mohair wig; white felt hat with felt flower on inside of rim and green ribbon ties. Her light green taffeta dress is three-quarter length; there is a felt flower and leaf on each side of lower skirt with one row of white lace around bottom. She also wears white pantaloons and black painted strapless slippers. *Jackie Robertson Collection.*

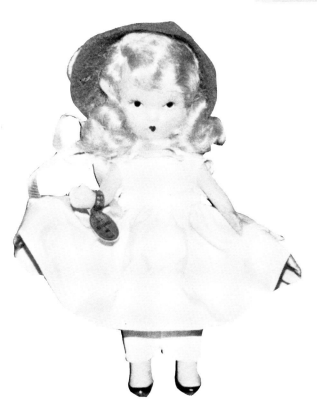

Illustration 264. *#121 He Loves Me, He Loves Me Not:* 5½in. (14cm) Bisque; blond mohair wig; magenta-colored felt hat with flowers. Doll wears short light pink taffeta dress with white lace trim, white underskirt, white pantaloons and black painted strapless slippers. *Shirley Nathan Collection. Photo by Howard Nathan.*

Illustration 265. #121 He Loves Me, He Loves Me Not: 5½in. (14cm) Bisque with frozen legs; dark mohair wig; white satin ribbon tied in bow around hair. Doll has a white taffeta bodice, long organdy dress with ½in. (12.7mm) lace around skirt and pink daisy on right side of waist. She also wears a white underslip, white pantaloons and black painted strapless slippers.

Illustration 266. #121 He Loves Me, He Loves Me Not: 5½in. (14cm) Painted bisque with frozen legs; dark mohair wig; yellow bow on each side of head. She wears a three-quarter length yellow taffeta dress with white lace trim at neck and around skirt and white daisy with yellow ribbon and bow on lace attached to right side of skirt. She also wears white pantaloons and black painted strapless slippers.

106

Illustration 267. Below. *#122 Alice, Sweet Alice:* 5½in. (14cm) Bisque with frozen legs; auburn mohair wig; small lace hat with red poppy on top and red ribbons. She wears a long multicolored taffeta dress (red-blue-green-yellow-white) with white scalloped trim around skirt. She also has white underslip, long pantaloons and black painted strapless slippers.

Illustration 268. Above. *#122 Alice, Sweet Alice:* 5½in. (14cm) Bisque with frozen legs; blond mohair wig; small black round hat with red poppy. Her dress has a bodice of red taffeta and short skirt in a red and white stripe. She also wears white pantaloons and black painted strapless slippers.

Illustration 269. #122 Alice, Sweet
Alice: 5½in. (14cm) Bisque with frozen
legs; red mohair wig; dark blue rounded
felt hat with red ribbon across top and
tied under chin. Doll wears red taffeta
bodice, short multicolored striped skirt
(red-white-yellow-blue-green), white pantaloons and black painted strapless
slippers.

Illustration 270. #122 Alice, Sweet Alice: 5¼in.
(13.1cm) Painted bisque with jointed arms and legs;
dark mohair wig; her poppy-like hat is missing. Doll has
dark red bodice, yellow net collar, short striped skirt
(blue-green-yellow-red-white), white pantaloons and
black painted strapless slippers.

Illustration 271. Left. #122 Alice, Sweet Alice:
5½in. (14cm) Bisque with frozen legs; dark mohair
wig; white net is gathered to form hat accented by
red ribbon streamers. She wears a long multicolored striped dress (red-white-blue-yellow)
which has wide white lace-like trim around skirt.
She also wears white pantaloons and black painted
strapless slippers.

Illustration 272. Above. *#124 Pretty As a Picture:* 5in. (12.7cm) Bisque with jointed arms and legs; dark mohair wig; light blue felt fitted hat with blue gathered organdy ruffle as trim and dark blue ribbon ties. Her short yellow cotton dress with small blue flower print has a blue organdy apron. She also wears pantaloons and black painted strapless slippers. *Pamela Ann Ford Collection.*

Illustration 273. Lower right. *#124 Pretty As a Picture:* 5½in. (14cm) Bisque with jointed arms and frozen legs; auburn mohair wig; peach ribbon tied in bow around hair. Her peach bodice has blue taffeta trim. her three-quarter length skirt is of blue taffeta and her peach apron has a white flower design with one row of gathered peach ribbon as trim. She also wears white pantaloons and black painted strapless slippers. *Jackie Robertson Collection.*

Illustration 274. Upper right. *#124 Pretty As a Picture:* 5½in. (14cm) Bisque with frozen legs; blond mohair wig; light pink felt hat with pink ribbon ties. Her short three quarter length pink taffeta dress has a red and blue flower and green leaf print. The bodice is of blue taffeta with pink cording across chest; the blue taffeta apron also has pink cording and light pink with blue embroidery thread trim at hemline. She also wears pantaloons and black painted strapless slippers .

Illustration 275. *#125 Alice Thru the Looking Glass:* The three dolls are 5½in. (14cm) painted bisque with frozen legs and black-painted strapless slippers. All have longer hair than the usual 5½in. (14cm) dolls. From left to right: Long blue taffeta dress with white lace trim on each side of bodice; blue organdy apron with white lace trim; black ribbon around hair. Three-quarter length light lavender dress with white lace across chest; white eyelet apron; blue ribbon around hair; this particular doll has bangs. Three-quarter length blue and white check cotton dress with white ribbon trim across chest; white organdy apron with two rows of black cording as trim; black ribbon around hair. *Jackie Robertson Collection. Photo by Frank Westphal.*

Illustration 276. *#125 Alice in Wonderland:* 5in. (12.7cm) Bisque with jointed arms and legs; blond mohair wig with black ribbon around hair. She wears a short blue cotton print dress with white satin ribbon trim on bodice and two black ribbons as trim around skirt. Her white organdy apron has white embroidered flower design. Her molded socks are colored to match her body color and she also wears short white panties and black painted slippers.

Illustration 277. *#125 Alice Thru the Looking Glass:* 5½in. (14cm) Painted bisque with frozen legs; blond mohair wig with bangs over forehead; dark blue ribbon around hair. She wears a three-quarter length blue taffeta dress with dark blue ribbon around waist and around skirt, accented by a pink eyelet apron. She also has white pantaloons and black painted strapless slippers.

Illustration 278. *#126 I Have A Little Pet:* 5in. (12.7cm) Bisque with jointed arms and legs; blond mohair wig with pink ribbon around hair tied in bow. Her short dress is of pink organdy and the white trim has pink ribbon interwoven through it. She also wears short lace-edged panties and white painted high shoes. Her pet is a cat fastened with pin to right side of dress (or it can be tied to wrist). The cat is white and of bendable "pipe cleaners" or chenille with a fuzzy tail, bright green eyes, whiskers, red mouth and pink ribbon on neck. *Jackie Robertson Collection. Photo by Frank Westphal.*

Illustration 279. *#126 Pussy Cat, Pussy Cat:* 5in. (12.7cm) Painted bisque with jointed arms and legs; dark mohair wig; blue ribbon tied in bow around hair. Doll's short cotton dress is pink with small white dots; her white organdy apron has white trim. She also wears short white panties and white painted high boots. Cat appears to be made of "pipe cleaners" or chenille, though he is fluffy. *Nancy Roeder Collection. Photo by Susan Deats.*

Illustration 280. *#126 I'm Going a-Milking:* 5½in. (14cm) Painted bisque with frozen legs; blond mohair wig; white lace hat with red bow on top. She wears a three-quarter length dark blue taffeta dress, a white and red striped taffeta apron trimmed in white and red at hemline, white pantaloons and black painted strapless slippers.

Illustration 281. *#126 I'm Going a-Milking:* 5½in. (14cm) Bisque with jointed arms and frozen legs; blond mohair wig; white organdy pointed hat with blue bow and blue trim. Doll wears a dark blue felt bodice with white trim forming vee and three-quarter length cotton blue and white striped skirt with blue ribbon trim. She also wears white pantaloons and black painted strapless slippers. *Jackie Robertson Collection.*

Illustration 282. *#126 I'm Going a-Milking:* 5½in. (14cm) Painted bisque with frozen legs; blond mohair wig; white organdy dutch-type hat with white and red trim. Doll's bodice and apron are of red taffeta; there is red and white trim crossed over chest and along hemline of apron. The three-quarter length skirt of small cotton check (tan and white) has red cording as trim around bottom. She also wears white pantaloons and black painted strapless slippers.

Illustration 283. *#126 I'm Going a-Milking :* 5½in. (14cm) Bisque with frozen legs; blond mohair wig; white felt hat accented by small white feather. Doll wears a short blue taffeta dress, a small apron of red and white stripes with white and red trim at bottom, white pantaloons and black painted strapless slippers.

Illustration 284. *#127 Merry Little Maid:* 5½in. (14cm) Bisque with frozen legs; blond mohair wig; large pink felt hat with white ribbon ties. Doll has pink taffeta bodice, long sheer-type skirt with one row of pink cording as trim and flowers attached to cording on right side. She also wears white pantaloons and black painted strapless slippers.

Illustration 286. *#128. Goldilocks & Baby Bear:* 5in. (12.7cm) Bisque with jointed arms and legs; blond mohair wig; yellow ribbon tied in bow around hair. Her dress is short and of red taffeta; her yellow-flowered bodice and apron have red trim. She also wears white pantaloons and black painted strapless slippers. Bear is made of "pipe-cleaners" or similar material; he is fuzzy, has a pronounced tail, a muzzle, two black felt ears, a black sequin-like nose, two black dots for eyes and a red dot as nose. *Jackie Robertson Collection. Photo by Frank Westphal.*

Illustration 285. *#128 Goldilocks & Baby Bear:* 5in. (12.7cm) Bisque with jointed arms and legs; blond mohair wig; yellow ribbon tied in bow around hair. Her yellow bodice is trimmed in dark maroon, her skirt is maroon accented by a yellow apron trimmed in darker maroon. She wears black painted strapless slippers. The off-white bear is made from fluffy material.

Illustration 287. *#128 Goldilocks:* 5½in. (14cm) Painted bisque with frozen legs· blond mohair wig; blue felt hat with white ribbon ties. Her three-quarter length dress has blue taffeta bodice with one row of white lace as trim, skirt of white organdy with small blue flower print and one row of white lace around hemline. She also has white pantaloons and black painted strapless slippers.

Illustration 288. *#128 Goldilocks:* 5½in. (14cm) Bisque with jointed arms and frozen legs; blond mohair wig; red ribbon tied in bow around hair. Doll's red taffeta bodice has white net with red trim across top; her three-quarter length white taffeta dress has small red dots. She also wears white pantaloons and black painted strapless slippers. *Jackie Robertson Collection.*

Illustration 289. *#128 Goldilocks:* 5½in. (14cm) Bisque with jointed arms and frozen legs; blond mohair wig; dark blue ribbon around hair tied in bow. Doll has dark blue taffeta bodice and apron with gold cording as trim, a three-quarter length yellow-gold taffeta skirt with dark blue ribbon trim, white pantaloons and black painted strapless shoes. *Jackie Robertson Collection.*

Illustration 290. *#128 Goldilocks:* 5½in. (14cm) Bisque with jointed arms and frozen legs; blond mohair wig; pink ribbon tied around hair in bow. Doll wears pink taffeta bodice, three-quarter length skirt of silk-type material with white flower design, pink cording and one row of white lace around skirt as trim. She also has white pantaloons and black painted strapless slippers. *Jackie Robertson Collection.*

117

Illustration 291. *#129 East Side, West Side:* 5in. (12.7cm) Bisque with jointed arms and legs; auburn mohair wig; straw hat. Doll wears black felt jacket, short red and white cotton dress, white pantaloons and black painted high boots. *Linda Aringdale Collection.*

Illustration 292. *#129 Annie at the Garden Gate:* 5½in. (14cm) Painted bisque with frozen legs; dark mohair wig; red bow and berries on left side of hair. She wears red taffeta bodice, short red and white cotton check skirt with white ribbon as trim, white pantaloons and black painted strapless slippers.

Illustration 293. *#129 Annie at the Garden Gate:* 5½in. (14cm) Bisque with frozen legs; auburn mohair wig; red berries and green leaf in hair secured by green ribbon bow. Her bodice is of white organdy with green thread design across chest; her short skirt is polished cotton. She also wears white pantaloons and black painted strapless slippers.

Illustration 294. Below. *#129 Annie at the Garden Gate:* 5½in. (14cm) Bisque body with hard plastic arms; red mohair wig; dark green ribbon tied in bow around hair. Her long green taffeta dress has red berries at right side of waist; she also wears a white apron of 2in. (5.1cm) eyelet, white underslip, white pantaloons and black painted strapless slippers.

Illustration 295. *#130 Dainty Dolly Pink and Blue:* 5½in. (14cm) Bisque with frozen legs; blond mohair wig; white felt hat with gathered pink ribbon inside rim. Her three-quarter length dress has bodice and skirt of pink taffeta. There is an overskirt, 1½in. (3.8cm) long, of blue organdy, white pantaloons and black painted strapless slippers.

Illustration 296. *#130 Dainty Dolly Pink and Blue:* 5½in. (14cm) Bisque with frozen legs and jointed arms; blond mohair wig; pink felt hat with blue and pink flowers on top and pink bow on left side. Her long blue taffeta dress has 2in. (5.1cm) of lace near the base of skirt; above this is lace trim of pink and blue flowers made of thread. She also wears white pantaloons and black painted strapless slippers. *Jackie Robertson Collection.*

Illustration 297. *#131 Elsie Marley Grown So Fine:* 5½in. (14cm) Bisque with jointed arms and frozen legs; red mohair wig; dark blue felt hat with white feather on right side and yellow ribbon ties. Doll's three-quarter length varied blue and yellow check taffeta dress has one row of white lace trim around skirt. Doll also wears white pantaloons and black painted strapless slippers. *Jackie Robertson Collection.*

Illustration 298. *#131 Elsie Marley Grown So Fine:* 5½in. (14cm) Bisque with jointed arms and frozen legs; red mohair wig; deep lavender fitted felt hat with large white feather. Her three-quarter length lavender dress has a white apron with two rows of red trim. Doll also wears white pantaloons and black painted strapless slippers.

Illustration 299. *#131 Elsie Marley Grown So Fine:* 5½in. (14cm) Bisque with jointed arms and legs; dark mohair wig; maroon felt hat with white feather. Her short off-white taffeta dress has small maroon dots and a 1½in. (3.8cm) overskirt. She also wears white pantaloons and black painted strapless slippers.

Illustration 300. *#132 When She Was Good She Was Very, Very Good:* 5½in. (14cm) Bisque with frozen legs; blond mohair wig; pink ribbon tied in a bow around hair. She wears a three-quarter length dress in small flower print with pink trim around skirt, white pantaloons and black painted strapless slippers.

Illustration 301. *#132 When She Was Good She Was Very, Very Good:* 5½in. (14cm) Painted bisque with frozen legs and hard plastic arms; blond mohair wig; pink ribbon tied in bow around hair. She wears a pink taffeta bodice, a white three-quarter length taffeta skirt with small pink flower print and pink gathered ribbon as trim. Doll also wears white pantaloons and black painted strapless slippers.

Illustration 303. *#134 Old Mother Hubbard.* 5in. (12.7cm) Bisque with jointed arms and legs; blond mohair wig with slight knob or bump and molded hair under wig; gathered white net hat with black ribbon. She wears a long polished cotton dress with white bodice and net sleeves; a gathered blue overskirt opens in center revealing a long white organdy apron with lace trim. Her lower skirt is blue with red and white designs and she also wears a white scarf with white net trim, a white underskirt and pantaloons. Her molded socks are painted to match the color of her body and she wears black painted strapless slippers.

(NOTE: A similar outfit without apron is used for the Colonial Dame and also the doll representing America in the *Around the World Series.) Christy Ackerman Collection.*

Illustration 302. *#132 When She Was Good She Was Very, Very Good:* 5½in. (14cm) Bisque with frozen legs; blond mohair wig; pink ribbon tied in bow around hair. Doll has pink taffeta bodice, pink taffeta skirt with red roses, white pantaloons with lace and black painted strapless slippers. *Carole Sladek Collection. Photo by Tod Sladek.*

Illustration 304. *#132 When She was Good She Was Very, Very Good:* 5½in. (14cm) Painted bisque with frozen legs blond mohair wig; pink felt hat with pink ribbon ties. Her long dress is of white marquisette material with pink trim around waist and skirt. She also wears white underslip, white pantaloons and black painted strapless slippers. *Susan Deats Collection.*

Illustration 305. *#135 Jack and Jill:* Both dolls are 5in. (12.7cm) bisques with jointed arms and legs; dark mohair wigs. Boy wears red polished cotton trousers, red polka dot cotton shirt (opening in back) and black bow tie. Girl wears a short red and white polka dot cotton dress, white pantaloons and black painted strapless slippers. Both have molded socks painted over to match color of body. *Jackie Robertson Collection. Photo by Frank Westphal.*

Illustration 306. *#135 Jack:* 5½in. (14cm) Painted bisque with frozen legs; short dark mohair wig. He wears a black felt jacket, blue cotton shirt with small clustered dots (white-yellow-blue-red), dark blue polished cotton trousers and black painted strapless slippers. *Nancy Roeder Collection. Photo by Susan Deats.*

Illustration 308. *#137 Topsy:* 5in. (12.7cm) Bisque with jointed arms and legs; molded hair beneath black mohair wig; three red bows in hair. Her short red and white checked dress has red ribbon belt around waist and trim on small white organdy apron. She also wears short white panties and black painted high shoes with four white dots representing buttons. She has molded socks painted over to match color of body and there is a gold "Nancy Ann" sticker on apron. Marked on back "JUDY//ANN//USA."

Illustration 307. Below. *#137 Topsy:* 5in. (12.7cm) Bisques with jointed arms and legs. Left: Black mohair wig over molded bangs; hair in three pigtails tied with red ribbon. Her short dress is of red and white checked cotton and she has a detachable white organdy apron with red ribbon ties. She also wears short white panties and black painted high-top shoes with four white dots representing buttons. Right: There are no molded bangs under wig; but she also has three pigtails tied with red ribbon. Her dress is short with large red and white checks (possibly she had an apron). She also wears short white panties and black painted high-top shoes with the white dots. (NOTE: Some of these dolls are marked on back: "JUDY//ANN//USA.") *Jackie Robertson Collection. Photo by Frank Westphal.*

125

Illustration 309. #139 Hansel and #140 Gretel: Both dolls are 5in. (12.7cm) bisques with jointed arms and legs and black painted strapless slippers. Left: Hansel wears black felt peaked hat with yellow ribbon ties, black cotton flower print shirt and green polished cotton trousers. Right: Gretel wears a red felt fitted hat with yellow ribbon ties, a green polished cotton three-quarter length dress with apron to match Hansel's shirt accented by one row of yellow ribbon as trim.

Illustration 310. #152 Mary Had a Little Lamb: 5½in. (14cm) Painted bisque with jointed arms and legs; dark mohair wig; peach felt hat with cloth flower on top and pink ribbon over top of hat which ties under chin. Doll wears long pale peach taffeta dress with small rose and leaf print, a white organdy apron with gathered pale pink organdy and pink ribbon as trim. There is also pink ribbon at waist tied in bow with streamers, white underslip, white pantaloons and black painted strapless slippers.

Illustration 311. Below. *#152 Mary Had a Little Lamb:* 5½in. (14cm) Painted bisque with frozen legs; red mohair wig; dark green felt hat with yellow ribbon ties. Doll wears long cotton dress in yellow and black small checks with one row of green cording across chest and two rows around skirt as trim. She also has white underslip, pantaloons and black painted strapless slippers.

Illustration 312. Above. *#152 Mary Had a Little Lamb:* 5in. (12.7cm) Bisque (pudgy tummy doll) with jointed arms and legs; dark mohair wig with two blue ribbon bows on either side; fairly large white felt bonnet with darker blue ribbon ties and lighter blue material flowers on inside right brim. Her ankle-length white taffeta dress has a small blue flower print; white trim with very narrow blue bias tape appears to be interwoven around waist. Doll also has white underslip, white pantaloons with lace trim and black painted strapless slippers. *Jackie Robertson Collection. Photo by Frank Westphal.*

Illustration 313. *#153 Little Bo Peep:* 5in. (12.7cm)Painted bisque with jointed arms and legs; blond mohair wig over molded, hair; small round pink felt hat with felt flowers on top. She wears a short pink organdy dress and overskirt of pink flower print. Her white underslip has lace trim as do her pantaloons. She has molded socks painted to match color of her body and black painted strapless slippers. White staff is tied to right wrist with blue ribbon.

Illustration 314. *#153 Little Bo Peep:* 5½in. (14cm) Bisque with frozen legs; blond mohair wig; pink felt bonnet. Her pink taffeta dress has a pink flowered overskirt and she wears white pantaloons and black painted strapless slippers. *Marian Schmuhl Collection.*

Illustration 315. *#153 Little Bo Peep:* 5½in. (14cm) Bisque with frozen legs; blond mohair wig; small flat felt headpiece with lavender flowers and ribbon over hat tied in bow in back. Doll wears a yellow taffeta long dress with small deep pink flower print; her 2in. (5.1cm) overskirt is lavender. There is a lavender bow at her waist, white underslip, white pantaloons and black painted strapless slippers.

Illustration 316. *#153 Little Bo Peep:* 5½in. (14cm) Painted bisque with frozen legs; blond mohair wig; small round blue felt hat with felt flowers and blue ribbon ties. Doll has a white sheer bodice and 2in. (5.1cm) overskirt of small blue flower print. Her long skirt is of white taffeta and has one row of white lace around bottom. She also wears a white underslip, white pantaloons and black painted strapless slippers.

Illustration 317. *#153 Little Bo Peep:* 5½in. (14cm) Bisque with frozen legs; blond mohair wig; pink circular felt hat with pink ribbon ties and felt flowers on top. Doll wears a white organdy flower print bodice and apron with white lace trim on sleeves and apron edge; her three-quarter length lavender taffeta skirt also has white lace trim. She wears white pantaloons and black painted strapless slippers. *Jackie Robertson Collection.*

Illustration 320. Below. *#154 Curly Locks:* 5½in. (12.7cm) Bisque with jointed arms and frozen legs; dark mohair wig; organdy Dutch-type hat with eyelet edging and pink ribbon ties. Her long white taffeta dress has small red dots; her apron is of white organdy embossed to give the appearance of trim. She also wears white pantaloons and black painted strapless slippers. *Jackie Robertson Collection.*

Illustration 318. *#154 Curly Locks:* 5in. (12.7cm) Bisque with jointed arms and legs; molded hair under blond mohair wig; blue ribbon tied in bow around hair. Doll wears light pink organdy dress with blue organdy apron which has flower ribbon trim. She also wears short white panties and black painted strapless slippers. Doll has the molded socks to match coloring of body. *Ann Blancherd Collection.*

Illustration 319. Left. *#154 Curly Locks:* 5½in. (14cm) Bisque with frozen legs; red mohair wig; lavender felt bow on right side of rim. Doll wears long maroon taffeta dress and white organdy apron; there are varying shades of maroon ribbon as trim on apron and across chest. She also has a white underslip, white pantaloons and black painted strapless slippers.

Illustration 321. *#154 Curly Locks:* 5½in. (14cm) Painted bisque with frozen legs; blond mohair wig; ½in. (12.1mm) white eyelet sewn onto white ribbon is tied around hair with bow at right side. Doll wears long lavender sheer dress with white flower and stem print trimmed in white lace around hemline. She also wears a small white eyelet apron, white underslip, white pantaloons and black painted strapless slippers.

Illustration 324. Below. *#155 Cinderella:* 5½in. (14cm) Painted bisque with frozen legs; blond mohair wig; pink bow on left side of hair. She wears a blue taffeta dress, a three-quarter length pink over-skirt gathered on each side accented by pink bows, white underslip, white pantaloons and black painted strapless slippers.

Illustration 322. *#155 Cinderella:* Early 5in. (12.7cm) bisque with jointed arms and legs; blond mohair wig; pink bow with three decorative "circles" along with flowers in hair. Doll wears long chiffon flocked two-piece effect skirt accented by felt flowers at right. Her slip is attached to waist and has lace trim. She also has white pantaloons with lace trim and silver painted strapless slippers.

Illustration 323. Left. *#155 Cinderella:* 5½in. (14cm) Painted bisque with frozen legs and hard plastic arms; blond mohair wig; pink ribbon around hair and large gold paper flower on top. Her long pink taffeta dress has wide lace-like trim interwoven with gold metallic thread and gold cording above this. She also wears a white underslip, white pantaloons and black painted strapless slippers.

Illustration 325. Right: *Snow White:* 5in. (12.7cm) Bisque with jointed arms and legs; dark brown mohair wig; tall peaked white taffeta hat with white net veil attached to right side of hat. Her bodice is white taffeta with net trim on sleeves; her overskirt is of white net and her underskirt is of white taffeta. She also wears white pantaloons with lace trim and black painted strapless slippers. *Anita P. Wright Collection.*

Illustration 327. Below. *#155 Cinderella:* 5½in. (14cm) Bisque with blond mohair wig; two pink hair ribbons. Doll wears a dress of pink taffeta with pink net overskirt, accented by pink and blue felt medallions. She also wears white pantaloons and black painted strapless slippers. *Shirley Nathan Collection.*

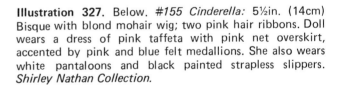

Illustration 326. Above. *#155 Cinderella:* 5in.(12.7cm) Bisque with jointed arms and legs; blond mohair wig; pink bow and flower in hair. Doll wears a dress of pink taffeta with blue flower print in which the sides are gathered. She also wears an underskirt of white net, underslip of white taffeta, white pantaloons and silver painted strapless slippers. *Jackie Robertson Collection.*

Illustration 328. #156 Beauty (from Beauty and the Beast): 5in. (12.7cm) Bisque with jointed arms and legs; dark mohair wig; blue ribbon tied in bow around hair. She wears a blue taffeta dress with flower print bodice and skirt that is gathered on each side to expose underslip with lace trim and flower. Doll has white half underslip, white pantaloons and black painted strapless slippers. *Jackie Robertson Collection.*

Illustration 329. #156 Beauty (from Beauty and the Beast): 5½in. (14cm) Bisque with frozen legs; red mohair wig; white feather and bow on left side of hair. Doll's long peach taffeta dress has a three-quarter length pink net overskirt and is gathered on each side with a trim of satin pink and blue ribbon. She also wears white underslip, white pantaloons and black painted strapless slippers.

Illustration 330. *#156 Beauty (from Beauty and the Beast):* 5½in. (14cm) bisque with frozen legs; dark mohair wig; white ribbon around hair with feather. Her long light lavender taffeta dress has white insert with braided flower design on each side of insert. Doll also has white half underslip, white pantaloons and black painted strapless slippers.

Illustration 331. *#156 Beauty (from Beauty and the Beast):* Both dolls are 5½in. (14cm) painted bisques with frozen legs and headdresses of circular blue felt with feathers and blue ribbon ties. Doll on left has brown eyes; doll on right has blue eyes. Their dresses are similar and of light blue taffeta with white flower flocking and white lace trim; doll on left has smaller flower on bodice than doll on right. In addition, both dolls have white pantaloons and black painted strapless slippers. *Jackie Robertson Collection. Photo by Frank Westphal.*

Illustration 332. *#157 Queen of Hearts:* 5½in. (14cm) Bisque with jointed arms and legs; dark mohair wig; white net hat with open crown. Doll wears red taffeta bodice and underskirt; her overskirt is of white organdy with a large red felt heart and ribbon bow on right side. She also wears long white pantaloons and black painted strapless slippers.

Illustration 333. *#157 Queen of Hearts:* 5½in. (14cm) Bisque with frozen legs; blond mohair wig; red felt fitted hat with peak on top, lace trim and red ribbon ties. She wears a long red taffeta dress with large organdy apron accented by two rows of eyelet-like trim. There is a red felt heart on right side of apron and doll wears white pantaloons and black painted strapless slippers.

Illustration 334. *#157 Queen of Hearts:* 5½in. (14cm) Bisque with frozen legs; dark mohair wig; red felt heart-shaped hat with red bow. Her red taffeta bodice contrasts with the white net skirt accented by large red heart and red bow on right side. There is a white underskirt, white pantaloons and black painted strapless slippers.

Illustration 335. *#157 Queen of Hearts:* 5½in. (14cm) Bisque with jointed arms and legs; brown mohair wig; net headdress. Her red taffeta dress has white organza overskirt, accented by red felt heart. She also wears white pantaloons and black painted strapless slippers. *Marian Schmuhl Collection.*

137

Illustration 336. Left. *#158 Sugar and Spice and Everything Nice:* 5½in. (14cm) Bisque with frozen legs; auburn mohair wig; white felt fitted hat with pink ribbon ties. Doll wears a long white organdy dress with white flower design and pink ribbon trim; the underskirt is of small red and white checks with two rows of white lace trim around bottom. Doll also wears white pantaloons and black painted strapless slippers. *Pamela Ann Ford Collection.*

Illustration 337. Right. *#158 Sugar and Spice and Everything Nice:* 5½in. (14cm) Bisque with jointed arms and frozen legs; blond mohair wig; blue ribbon tied in bow around hair. Her long pink taffeta dress is in a blue-yellow-pink-white flower print; there is blue satin ribbon around waist tied in bow at back. Doll also wears white pantaloons and black painted strapless slippers. *Jackie Robertson Collection.*

Illustration 338. Left. *#158 Sugar and Spice and Everything Nice:* 5½in.(14cm) Bisque with jointed arms and frozen legs; auburn mohair wig; fitted dark blue felt hat with blue ribbon ties. Doll wears long white organdy dress with flower print and dark blue fringe as trim across chest and around skirt. In addition she has white pantaloons and black painted strapless slippers. *Jackie Robertson Collection.*

Illustration 339. Right. *#158 Sugar and Spice and Everything Nice:* 5½in. (14cm) Bisque with frozen legs; blond mohair wig; pink ribbon tied in bow around hair. She wears a long pink organdy dress with pink ribbon trim and pink satin ribbon around waist, white underslip, white pantaloons and black painted strapless slippers. *Jackie Robertson Collection.*

Illustration 340. Below. *#158 Sugar and Spice and Everything Nice:* 5½in. (14cm) Painted bisque with frozen legs; dark mohair wig; red satin ribbon tied in bow around hair. She wears a long plaid (red-green-blue-yellow-green) taffeta dress with white organdy apron which has red and white trim and white lace. She also has white underslip, white pantaloons and black painted strapless slippers. On box was written "Boston Store $1.58."

Illustration 342. #159 *Ring Around a Rosy, Pocket Full of Posy:* 5½in. (14cm) Bisque with frozen legs; blond mohair wig; lavender ribbon tied in bow around hair. Her dress is of white taffeta in small rose print, her white organdy apron has a pocket filled with posies and white organdy gathered trim along bottom. She also wears cotton underslip, white pantaloons and black painted strapless slippers.

Illustration 343. *#159 Ring Around a Rosy, Pocket Full of Posy:* 5½in. (14cm) Bisque with frozen legs; blond mohair wig; pink ribbon tied in bow around hair. Doll wears long light peach taffeta dress with small blue flower print trimmed in deep pink across bodice and around skirt. The pocket on right side of skirt has pink flowers. She also wears a white taffeta under-slip, white pantaloons and black painted strapless slippers.

Illustration 344. *#159 Ring Around a Rosy, Pocket Full of Posy:* 5½in. (14cm) Bisque with dark brown mohair wig; felt flowers in hair. Doll's dress is bright green with clear checked plastic apron and felt flowers in pocket. She also wears an underskirt, white panta-loons and black painted strapless slippers. *Shirley Nathan Collection. Photo by Howard Nathan.*

Illustration 345. *#160 Pretty Maid:* 5in. (12.7cm) Bisque with jointed arms and legs; blond mohair wig; pink felt hat with blue feather. She wears a white taffeta dress in flower print; it has a two-tier skirt with pink loop trim accented with pink and blue ribbons at waist. Her white cotton underslip is trimmed with lace and attached to waist. She also wears white pantaloons with lace trim and black painted strapless slippers.

Illustration 346. *#160 Pretty Maid:* 5½in. (14cm) Bisque with jointed arms and legs; blond mohair wig; blue felt hat with flowers. Doll's bodice is of blue taffeta with two rows of pink cording as trim on each side. She also wears a white seersucker flower print skirt with pink ribbon trim, a yellow taffeta underskirt, white pantaloons and black painted strapless slippers.

Illustration 347. *#160 Pretty Maid:* 5½in. (14cm) Painted bisque with frozen legs; blond mohair wig; pink felt hat with white cloth flower on inside rim and pink ribbon ties. She wears a long white organdy dress with pink ribbon around waist and 1in. (2.5cm) white lace trim at lower skirt — each end has a pink bow. She also wears white underslip, white pantaloons and black painted strapless slippers.

Illustration 348. *#160 Pretty Maid:* 5½in. (14cm) Painted bisque with frozen legs; blond mohair wig; small peach felt hat with peach ribbon ties. Doll wears three-quarter length light peach taffeta dress, an overksirt of peach organdy with small flower design and gathered peach ribbon as trim. She also has white pantaloons and black painted strapless slippers.

Illustration 350. *#161 Jennie Set the Table:* 5½in. (14cm) Painted bisque with frozen legs; dark mohair wig; red satin ribbon tied in bow around hair. Doll wears a long plaid cotton dress (red-white-green-black), white organdy apron with wide red ribbon and white lace as trim, white underslip and pantaloons and black painted strapless slippers.

Illustration 351. *#161 Jennie Set the Table:* 5½in. (14cm) Bisque with frozen legs; auburn mohair wig; piece of white lace across head. Doll wears a green top and apron with three rows of yellow trim and white lace along the bottom. Her yellow skirt is a print with blue red, green and yellow flowers. She also wears a white underskirt and black painted strapless slippers. *Marjorie Smith Collection.*

Illustration 352. *#161 Jennie Set the Table:* 5½in. (14cm) Bisque with frozen legs; red mohair wig; white eyelet hat with green bow on top. Doll wears a long checked taffeta dress with white eyelet apron, white pantaloons and black painted strapless slippers.

145

Illustration 353. *#162 Princess Rosanie:* 5½in. (14cm) Painted bisque with jointed arms and legs; dark mohair wig; crown made of embroidery-type small circles sewn to blue ribbon tied in back with bow. Her long taffeta peach flower print dress has a double center panel, one of plain peach taffeta, the other of chiffon with flocking of large circular design . It is edged at the base of the panel in trim that matches the crown. In addition, a pink and blue trim extends around the rest of the skirt. Doll also wears pantaloons with lace trim and black painted strapless slippers.

Illustration 354. *#162 Princess Rosanie:* 5½in. (14cm) Bisque with jointed arms and frozen legs; blond mohair wig; lavender ribbon tied around hair in bow. Doll is dressed in long light lavender taffeta small flower print dress with pink ribbon trim around bottom. She also wears a sheer overskirt gathered at each side and decorated with white flowers at gathered sides. *Jackie Robertson Collection.*

Illustration 355. *#162 Princess Rosanie:* 5½in. (14cm) Painted bisque with frozen legs; dark mohair wig; deep pink satin ribbon around hair. Her long deep pink marquisette dress has two rows of white lace trim and a large bow of deep pink satin ribbon with streamers at right side of waist. Doll also wears white underslip and pantaloons and black painted strapless slippers.

Illustration 356. *#162 Princess Rosanie:* 5in. (12.7cm) Bisque with jointed arms and legs; blond mohair wig; pink crocheted crown. Doll wears long off-white taffeta dress with flower, white line and white dot design. Her overskirt is of the same material, trimmed the same as the bottom edge of her skirt in pink. There are pink and white ribbon streamers at center of waist, and she also wears white pantaloons and black painted strapless slippers. *Jackie Robertson Collection.*

Illustration 357. *#162 Princess Rosanie:* 5½in. (14cm) Painted bisque with frozen legs; blond mohair wig; pink ribbon around hair. Her long white taffeta dress has a small rose flower print, center panel of organdy in white flower print trimmed with a row of white lace on either side, pink bow on right side of skirt and pink gathered ribbon around base of skirt. She also wears white underslip and pantaloons and black painted strapless slippers.

147

Illustration 358. *#163 Little Miss Donnet, She Wore a Big Bonnet:* 5½in. (14cm) Painted bisque with frozen legs; dark mohair wig; large red felt hat with red ribbon gathered on inside of rim. Doll wears red taffeta bodice, sheer white skirt with large red dot print, red taffeta underskirt, white pantaloons and black painted strapless slippers.

Illustration 359. *#163 Little Miss Donnet, She Wore a Big Bonnet:* 5½in. (14cm) Painted bisque with jointed arms and legs; blond mohair wig; large light blue felt hat with pink ribbon gathered to form trim along inside. Her blue taffeta bodice is attached to a skirt of blue with flower print and overskirt of dimity with white dot flocking. She also wears a white underslip, pantaloons with white lace trim and black painted strapless slippers.

Illustration 360. *#163 Little Miss Donnet, She Wore a Big Bonnet:* 5½in. (14cm) Bisque with frozen legs; red mohair wig; blue felt hat with gathered pink ribbon on inside of rim. Doll wears a pink taffeta bodice with light pink heavy cotton long skirt trimmed in blue. She also has white long pantaloons and black painted strapless slippers.

Illustration 361. *#163 Little Miss Donnet, She Wore a Big Bonnet:* 5¼in. (13.3cm) Painted bisque with jointed legs; blond mohair wig; large blue felt hat with gathered peach ribbon trim on inside of hat. Her long, full off-white taffeta dress has a small flower flocking pattern with peach ribbon and eyelet trim around skirt. She wears a peach ribbon around waist, tied in back. She also wears white pantaloons and black painted strapless slippers.

Illustration 362. *#163 Little Miss Donnet, She Wore a Big Bonnet:* 5½in. (14cm) Bisque with frozen legs; blond mohair wig; large dark blue felt bonnet with gathered peach ribbon sewn along inside of rim and blue ribbon ties. Doll wears a long heavy cotton blue dress accented by one row of dark blue cording across bodice and two rows around skirt. She also wears long white pantaloons and black painted strapless slippers.

Illustration 363. *#163 Little Miss Donnet, She Wore a Big Bonnet:* 5½in. (14cm) Bisque with frozen legs; auburn mohair wig; large red felt hat with gathered red ribbon on inside rim and red ribbon ties. She wears a red taffeta bodice and a long white cotton skirt with red dots and two rows of red cord as trim around skirt. In addition, she wears white underskirt, white pantaloons and black painted strapless slippers. *Jackie Robertson Collection.*

Illustration 364. *#163 Little Miss Donnet, She Wore a Big Bonnet:* 5½in. (14cm) Bisque with frozen legs; auburn mohair wig; magenta felt hat. Doll wears a plaid taffeta dress with white lace, white underslip, white pantaloons and black painted strapless slippers. *Shirley Nathan Collection. Photo by Howard Nathan.*

Illustration 365. *#168 Silks and Satins:* 5½in. (14cm) Bisque with jointed arms and frozen legs; blond mohair wig; gold braid sewn to wide pink satin ribbon, tied around hair with large bow on right side. Her dress is of satin-type material in pink with one row of white lace and gold cording around skirt. Doll also wears white pantaloons and black painted strapless slippers. *Jackie Robertson Collection Photo by Richard Howard.*

150

Illustration 366. *#169 Goose Girl:* 5½in. (14cm) Bisque with frozen legs; long blond mohair wig, parted in center; ribbons tied onto each side of hair; white organdy cap. Her red bodice is cotton and is accented by white cording in crisscross design and her long blue cotton skirt has one row of red cording as trim. She also wears a white organdy apron with red ribbon trim, pantaloons and black painted strapless slippers.

Illustration 367. *#169 Goose Girl:* 5½in. (14cm) Painted bisque with frozen legs; long blond mohair wig parted in center; two red bows in hair. Doll's black felt bodice has white lace trim at neck and around sleeves and trim of orange cording is crossed over chest. Her long red polished cotton skirt has white organdy apron trimmed in yellow and brown cording and 1¼in. (3.1cm) white trim along edge. She also wears a white underslip, pantaloons and black painted strapless slippers.

Illustration 368. *#169 Goose Girl:* 5½in. (14cm) Bisque with frozen legs; blond mohair wig; white lace-like hat with cluster of pink flowers. Her light green bodice has pink trim sewn in vee , her skirt is pink and green taffeta trimmed in pink cording. She also wears a white lace-like apron with cluster of flowers, white underslip, pantaloons and black painted strapless slippers.

Illustration 369. *#170 Rain, Rain Go Away:* 5½in. (14cm) Painted bisque with jointed arms and frozen legs; blond mohair wig; light blue ribbon tied in bow around hair. Doll wears a sheer long skirt with large blue flowers and small leaf design; her underskirt is of white taffeta. She also has white pantaloons, an umbrella of blue taffeta with gathered ruffle on top and black painted strapless slippers.

Illustration 371. *#170 Rain, Rain Go Away:* 5½in. (14cm) Bisque with frozen legs; blond mohair wig; royal blue felt hat with pointed tip. Doll wears matching royal blue cape over white with blue dotted swiss dress trimmed in two rows of blue cording. She also wears white pantaloons and black painted strapless slippers. *Jackie Robertson Collection. Photo by Richard Howard.*

Illustration 370. *#170 Rain, Rain Go Away:* 5½in. (14cm) Bisque with frozen legs; red mohair wig; blue ribbon tied in bow around hair. Her dress is a long blue taffeta one with two rows of yellow ribbon around skirt as trim. She also wears a yellow plastic cape and there is a matching umbrella tied to her wrist. She wears white pantaloons and black painted slippers.

Illustration 372. *#170 Rain, Rain Go Away:* 5½in. (14cm) Bisque with frozen legs; blond mohair wig; pink felt hat with pink fringe. Doll's long gray taffeta dress has pink fringe trim around skirt and her umbrella is also of gray taffeta with pink fringe trim and pink bow. Doll also wears white half slip, white pantaloons and black painted strapless slippers. *Jackie Robertson Collection.*

Illustration 373. *#170 Rain, Rain Go Away:* 5½in. (14cm) Painted bisque with frozen legs; blond mohair wig; 1½in. (3.8cm) wide gathered peach taffeta material sewn to peach ribbon and tied in bow at back of head. Doll's long tan taffeta dress has peach ribbon trim across bodice and around lower skirt. There is a matching umbrella of peach taffeta with bow tied to her wrist. She also wears a white underslip, pantaloons and black painted strapless slippers.

Illustration 374. Left. *#171 Daffy-Down-Dilly:* 5½in. (14cm) Bisque with frozen legs; blond mohair wig; large yellow felt hat with gathered yellow ribbon around outside rim. Doll wears a bodice of yellow taffeta, a long yellow organdy-like skirt with small dot flocking and yellow satin ribbon around skirt as trim. She also wears a green taffeta underskirt, white pantaloons and black painted strapless slippers.

Illustration 375. Right. *#171 Daffy-Down-Dilly:* 5½in. (14cm) Bisque with frozen legs; dark mohair wig; wide yellow gathered ribbon forms headdress with open crown and yellow ribbon ties. Doll wears yellow taffeta bodice, organdy skirt with white flower design and gathered yellow ribbon as trim accented by two yellow bows. She also has a green taffeta underskirt, white pantaloons and black painted strapless slippers. *Jackie Robertson Collection. Photo by Frank Westphal.*

Illustration 376. *#172 The Snow Queen:* 5½in. (14cm) Bisque with frozen legs; blond mohair wig; white satin ribbon around hair with large white flower on right side. Her dress is white and there is an overskirt of net with wide border of embroidery-like trim. She also wears white pantaloons and black painted strapless slippers.

Illustration 377. *#172 The Snow Queen:* (Left) 5½in. (14cm) Bisque with frozen legs; blond mohair wig; gold paper crown with net veil. Doll wears a white taffeta bodice, a skirt of white organdy with flower design and 2in. (5.1cm) overskirt of ecru-colored lace, underslip of taffeta trimmed with white lace, white pantaloons and black painted strapless slippers. (Right) 5½in. (14cm) Bisque with frozen legs; blond mohair wig; white lace headband. Doll wears a dress of white taffeta with 2in. (5.1cm) of net trim around skirt with interwoven gold threads, white pantaloons and black painted strapless slippers. *Jackie Robertson Collection. Photo by Frank Westphal.*

Illustration 378. *#172 The Snow Queen:* 5½in. (14cm) Bisque with frozen legs; light blond mohair wig; lace bandeau in hair. Doll wears satin dress with off-white net overskirt trimmed with lace, white underslip, white pantaloons and black painted strapless slippers. *Shirley Nathan Collection. Photo by Howard Nathan.*

Illustration 381. Below. *#173 Polly Put The Kettle On:* 5½in. (14cm) Painted bisque with frozen legs; blond mohair wig; eyelet hat. Her blue taffeta dress with large white dot print has a white apron with narrow dark blue cording as trim, and eyelet runs along edge of apron. She also wears white pantaloons and black painted strapless slippers. *Gloria J. Haley Collection.*

Illustration 379. *#173 Polly Put the Kettle On:* 5½in. (14cm) Bisque with jointed arms and frozen legs; blond mohair wig; pink trimmed white ribbon around hair tied in bow. Doll wears a bodice of white organdy with pink trim across chest, a light lavender taffeta skirt and white organdy apron with pink and blue design on ribbon trim. In addition she has white pantaloons and black painted strapless slippers. *Jackie Robertson Collection.*

Illustration 380. *#173 Polly Put the Kettle On:* 5½in. (14cm) Painted bisque with frozen legs; blond mohair wig; 1in. (2.5cm) white eyelet sewn on pink satin ribbon tied in back for headdress. She wears a long taffeta checked dress (blue-pink-white) with white cotton eyelet apron, white slip, white pantaloons and black painted strapless slippers.

Illustration 382. *#173 Polly Put the Kettle On:* 5½in. (14cm) Bisque with jointed arms and frozen legs; blond mohair wig; red ribbon and white eyelet for headdress. She wears a long black taffeta dress and white eyelet apron with large red ribbon bow on right side, white pantaloons and black painted strapless slippers. *Jackie Robertson Collection. Photo by Richard Howard.*

Illustration 383. *#173 Polly Put the Kettle On:* 5½in. (14cm) Painted bisque with frozen legs; dark mohair wig; red and white checked ribbon around hair. Her bodice is red and white checked. The long red taffeta skirt has white dotted swiss-type apron with one row of red and white checked material to match bodice as trim. She also wears white underskirt, pantaloons and black painted strapless slippers.

157

Illustration 384. *#173 Star Light, Star Bright;* 5½in. (14cm) Bisque body with hard plastic arms; golden blond mohair wig. Doll's long light blue gown is highlighted by tiny silver dots and silver and lace trim around skirt. Her cape is of light blue net, edged in white lace with ties of silver cording, and she also wears white pantaloons and black painted strapless slippers. A wand with star at top is tied to right wrist. *Jackie Robertson Collection. Photo by Richard Howard.*

Illustration 385. *#174 Florie Came from Dublin Town:* 5½in. (14cm) Bisque with frozen legs; auburn mohair wig; deep pink felt hat with pink flower and sheer bow. Her dress is sheer lavender with pink and white flowers and green leaves printed on in dot design, accented by lace trim and narrow pink cording. She also wears a white taffeta slip, white cotton pantaloons and black painted strapless slippers. *Carole Sladek Collection. Photo by Tod Sladek.*

Illustration 386. *#174 Flossie Came from Dublin Town:* 5½in. (14cm) Bisque with frozen legs; dark mohair wig; black felt hat with feather. Doll wears an aqua and peach taffeta dress, white pantaloons and black painted strapless slippers. *Shirley Nathan Collection. Photo by Howard Nathan.*

Illustration 387. *#175 There Was a Maiden Bright and Gay:* 5½in. (14cm) Painted bisque with frozen legs; dark mohair wig; white satin ribbon tied in bow around hair. Doll wears bodice of blue taffeta, white ribbon around waist, a chiffon skirt of light blue with white flower design and border of white satin ribbon and thread around skirt as trim. She also wears white underslip, pantaloons and black painted strapless slippers.

Illustration 388. *#175 There Was a Maiden Bright and Gay:* 5½in. (14cm) Bisque with frozen legs; blond mohair wig; felt pink flowers on ribbon around hair. Doll wears long nylon-type white dress with white flower print and light pink taffeta panel insert with white lace trim on either side. She also wears white half slip, white pantaloons and black painted strapless slippers. *Jackie Robertson Collection. Photo by Frank Westphal.*

Illustration 389. *#176 Nellie Bird, Nellie Bird:* 5½in. (14cm) Bisque with frozen legs; red mohair wig; purple taffeta is gathered and sewn to light blue ribbon as headdress. Her long purple taffeta dress has an a attached long apron of soft blue and yellow flowered cotton; there is a repeat of purple gathered taffeta as one row of trim on apron. In addition she wears white pantaloons and black painted strapless slippers. There is a broom tied to her right wrist with blue ribbon. *Jackie Robertson Collection. Photo by Frank Westphal.*

Illustration 390. Right. *#177 See-Saw Marjorie Daw:* 5½in. (14cm) Painted bisque with frozen legs; blond mohair wig; small round blue felt hat with blue feather and pink bow on right side. Doll wears a pink cotton dress with panel of lighter pink taffeta in flower print. She also wears a white underskirt, pantaloons and black painted strapless slippers.

Illustration 391. Left. *#177 See-Saw Marjorie Daw:* 5½in. (14cm) Bisque with frozen legs; blond mohair wig; shocking pink felt hat with white trim, pink ribbon and flower on right side. Doll wears long shocking pink nylon dress with white lace around bottom as trim. She also wears white underslip, white pantaloons and black painted strapless slippers. *Marjorie Smith Collection.*

Illustration 392. *#178 Gerda and Kay:* Both are 5in. (12.7cm) bisques with jointed arms and legs; blond mohair wigs and black painted strapless slippers; circa 1941. Left: Girl has dark blue bow on each side of head, a bodice and apron of black cotton with small flower print trimmed in two rows of pink. Beneath she wears a short gray polished cotton skirt and white pantaloons. Right: Boy has top made of gray polished cotton, pleated in center with two rows of pink ribbon across chest. His pants are black with flower print. *Jackie Robertson Collection. Photo by Richard Howard.*

Illustration 393. *#178 Give Me a Lassie as Sweet as She's Fair:* 5½in. (14cm) Bisque with jointed arms and frozen legs; dark mohair wig; large white feather and ribbon on left side of hair. Her long pink taffeta dress has white embossed-like flower design, accented by white trim across chest and around skirt. Doll also wears white half slip, white pantaloons and black painted strapless slippers. (NOTE: The white feather in hair is a similarity shared by all bisque *Lassies.*) *Jackie Robertson Collection.*

Illustration 394. *#178 Give Me a Lassie as Sweet as She's Fair:* 5½in. (14cm) Painted bisque with frozen legs; dark mohair wig; large white feather over top of head and white ribbon bow on right side. Doll's maroon taffeta bodice is attached to long white dotted swiss-type skirt with two maroon bows at hemline. She also wears a white underslip, pantaloons and black painted strapless slippers.

162

Illustration 395. #178 Give Me a Lassie as Sweet as She's Fair: 5½in. (14cm) Bisque with frozen legs; dark mohair wig; large white feather in hair. Her long taffeta checked dress (various shades of brown and white) has lace across bodice and around skirt as trim. She also wears white underslip, white pantaloons and black painted strapless slippers. *Jackie Robertson Collection. Photo by Frank Westphal.*

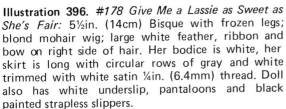

Illustration 396. #178 Give Me a Lassie as Sweet as She's Fair: 5½in. (14cm) Bisque with frozen legs; blond mohair wig; large white feather, ribbon and bow on right side of hair. Her bodice is white, her skirt is long with circular rows of gray and white trimmed with white satin ¼in. (6.4mm) thread. Doll also has white underslip, pantaloons and black painted strapless slippers.

Illustration 397. #179 Daisy Belle, Daisy Belle: 5½in. (14cm) Bisque with dark mohair wig; bright pink ribbon tied in bow around hair. Doll wears bright pink bodice, pink taffeta skirt with pink net overskirt accented by pink flower. She also has white underskirt, white pantaloons and black painted strapless slippers. *Ginny Zeidler Collection.*

Illustration 398. *#179 Daisy Belle, Daisy Belle:* 5½in. (14cm) Bisque with frozen legs; auburn mohair wig; small tan circular hat with ribbon trim extending over to right side. Doll's long tan taffeta dress has rose and tan organdy ribbon across bodice and around skirt. She also wears white underskirt, white pantaloons and black painted strapless slippers.

Illustration 399. *#179 The Babes in the Woods:* Both are 5in. (12.7cm) bisques with jointed arms and legs; dark mohair wigs; black painted strapless slippers. Girl has red and white checked peaked hat with red felt trim and red satin ribbon ties. Her dress is red and white checked with small patch on right side of skirt and she also wears white cotton pantaloons. Boy on left wears outfit of the same red and white checked material with patch on trousers. He has a red felt collar with red ribbon ties.

Valentine Sweetheart

Illustration 400. *Valentine Sweetheart.* (This doll did not have a number): 5½in. (14cm) Painted bisque with frozen legs; blond mohair wig; red felt hat with open crown, red ribbon ties and white feather on right side. Her short red taffeta dress has white lace trim around skirt and bodice as well as a white felt heart on left side of chest. She also wears red taffeta panties and black painted strapless slippers.

Furniture Series

Illustration 401. *#1008 Bed— #1009 Dressing Table, Mirror and Stool:* The furniture has a cardboard base, covered with pink taffeta in flower print design and stuffed with cotton for bed and stool. The dressing table has pink net between two gathered ruffles. The pink ribbon bows were added as trim. This furniture was discontinued after only a few years because of the amount of time necessary to make such items. In 1940 these types of furniture patterns were made available by the McCall Corporation (copyright applied for in 1940-#1,387,723 and #1,527, 518; McCall Printed Pattern #811). *Carol Westphal Collection. Photo by Frank Westphal.*

V. Plastic & Vinyl Dolls

Illustration 402. These are the hard plastic dolls with painted features, movable head, arms and legs (with the exception of the 3½ and 4in. (8.9 and 10.2cm) sizes -- they did not have the movable heads). All are 3½ to 7in. (8.9 to 17.8cm) and obtained from the original pamphlet enclosed within each doll's box. Note that some dolls which appeared in the bisque listing (pages 14-16) are missing from this list, as entire series and/or particular dolls were dropped with the production of plastic Nancy Ann Storybook Dolls. List dates from circa 1948.

Nancy Ann Storybook Dolls produced hard plastic dolls from 1948-1950. As with the bisque dolls, features on the hard plastics are hand-painted (excluding, of course, the eyes which were sleep-type). Thus, finding two exactly alike is unlikely. The hard plastic dolls have movable arms, legs and heads with the exception of the dolls in the 3½ to 4½in. (8.9cm to 11.5cm) sizes; the heads on these are molded as part of the entire body. All hard plastics have jointed arms and legs.

Hard plastic Nancy Ann Storybook Dolls are, of course, less fragile in comparison with the bisque dolls. In my opinion, the hard plastics lack the small girl appearance evident in the earlier bisques. However, at the time these hard plastics were being produced, competitors were bringing out adult-looking dolls, and perhaps this explains the "missing" little girl appearance of hard plastics.

Hard plastics are marked STORYBOOK// DOLLS// U.S.A.//TRADEMARK//REG.

There was a time when "The Doll Lady" offered dolls other than the 3½ to 7in. (8.9 to 17.8cm) storybook-types. In 1942, "Great Big Beautiful Dolls by Nancy Ann" were available at the City of Paris Store, Union Square, San Francisco. They were as lovely as any of the gorgeous dolls that used to come from France, dressed in rich materials, laces, ribbons and bonnets with flowers. They have human hair and range in size from 18 to 22in. (45.7 to 55.9cm). Originally, they were priced from $6.95 to $11.95. The 22in. (55.9cm) doll called *Little Rosebud* was dressed as a little girl in short dress, socks, flat shoes with three buttons and large bonnet-type hat. These dolls were discontinued

Illustration 403. These are the hard plastic dolls with sleep eyes, movable head, arms and legs (again, with the exception of the 3½ to 4½in. (8.9 to 11.5cm) sizes -- they did not have the movable heads). All are 3½ to 7in. (8.9 to 17.8cm) and obtained from the original pamphlet enclosed within each doll's box. List dates from circa 1950.

since the cost of their production was too high.

In 1950, the stunningly beautiful *Style Doll* was presented, representing a child dressed in make believe grown-up fashion. Each doll is as splendid as the next, made of plastic with saran wig, movable head, arms and legs. Style Dolls are exquisitely dressed in gowns of long taffeta, silk and nylon with embroidered nets and imported French laces. Trimmings include sequins, nosegays of flowers and ribbons. Neither doll nor clothing are marked, although there was a silver wrist tag on each doll that opened, 1½ x 2in. (3.8 x 5.1cm), marked on the outside "Style Show by Nancy Ann" and the name of the doll; inside there was a list of other Style Dolls available. Again, this doll was only made for a few years, for the cost of production also proved to be too high. Nancy Ann Abbott would not compromise for quality; she felt that if she could not offer the very best, she did not want it to be sold at all. (Note: There have been a few Nancy Ann Style Doll collectors who state the Style Doll was also sold with a hard plastic body and a vinyl head with rooted hair. No former employees of Nancy's are in agreement

with the above statement. Perhaps the tag of Nancy's Style Doll had been placed on another doll with such features by mistake.)

Reportedly in 1950, the hard plastic Nancy Ann Storybook dolls with sleep eyes began being produced. The first such dolls in sizes 3½ to 7in. (8.9 to 17.8cm) had pupilless eyes. These dolls have movable arms, legs and head with the exception of the dolls in the 3½ and 4½ in. (8.9 and 11.5cm) sizes and are also marked "STORY BOOK// DOLLS//U.S.A.// TRADEMARK//REG". A limited number of the 5½in. (14cm) dolls were made with a walking mechanism. These dolls have a mohair wig with the exception of the babies, which have molded hair. By 1953, these dolls had pupils in their eyes.

The 8in. (20.3cm) chubby *Muffie* made its appearance in the early 1950s (ca. 1953). Made of hard plastic, Muffie came with panties, shoes and socks. Extra outfits, hangers for same, hat, purse and pajamas, wardrobe trunk and other accessories were also sold separately for Muffie. In addition, Muffie had her own little pet dog. Her wig at first was saran, later dynel. Reportedly, the majority of

Illustrations 404a and 404b. These dolls are not to be confused with the original Nancy Ann Dolls created by Miss Abbott. The dolls of this type were presented by Mr. Albert M. Bourla for the first time at the New York Toy Fair in 1967. The outfits were made in Hong Kong for a completely redesigned line of Storybook Dolls. The packaging was also somewhat different with cellophane giving a window-type effect, although some dolls still came in the boxes with white backgrounds and various colored dots, boxes with "Nancy Ann" written on them and other styles. This company has discontinued selling dolls, but stockholders still exist. *Illustration 404a* shows Muffie; *Illustration 404b* shows March. Both from *Marge Meisinger Collection.*

Muffies had the straight walker-type legs with doll's head turning from side to side. Muffie was also made with bendable knees. The later Muffies had been available with hard plastic body and vinyl head with rooted hair. Muffies are found to be marked either just "Muffie" or, more frequently, "STORYBOOK // DOLLS // CALIFORNIA // MUFFIE."

Debbie soon followed (ca. 1954) as Muffie's big sister. She is 10in. (25.4cm) tall with straight walker-type legs, and her head moves from side to side; later she had a vinyl head with rooted hair and bendable knees. Many outfits were offered for Debbie, most of them copies of Muffie's. She is marked on the back of neck "NANCY ANN."

Next came *Lori Ann,* an 8in. (20.3cm) doll with hard plastic body and vinyl head with rooted hair. Again, there were many outfits offered for her and she is marked on the back of the neck, "NANCY ANN."

In 1957 the plastic body and vinyl head with rooted hair dolls with a more mature look were presented. *Miss Nancy Ann* is 10½in. (26.7cm) tall, has lifelike skin texture, swivel waist, movable arms, legs, sleep eyes, earrings and feet molded for high-heels. She is marked on the back of her neck "NANCY ANN." *Miss Nancy,* the small 8in. (20.3cm) doll, is similar to Miss Nancy Ann, but does not have the swivel waist or earrings. Miss Nancy is not marked, although her clothing is marked "By Nancy Ann Storybook Dolls Inc." The outfits for each of these dolls were made with care and forethought.

Finally, in the later 1950s, *Sue Sue* was offered. She was a 9in. (22.9cm) vinyl head with molded hair named after Les' wife. This cuddly baby came with a wide choice of lovely outfits, from pajamas to Sunday's Best. Each Sue Sue came dressed in a diaper with two snaps; many other outfits for her were sold separately.

It should be noted that reportedly in 1957 Nancy's company was in need of money, and to obtain additional funds they sold the first bisque mold (5in. or 12.7cm tall, slight knob on head beneath molded hair, molded socks) to a Japanese company. This Japanese company (name unknown) sold these dolls in the United States, also calling them Storybook Dolls. In fact, there were a number of companies in the United States that tried to sell their dolls as Storybook Dolls; they were sent a letter explaining they could not be permitted to do so, and in some cases, it was necessary to go to court. *For subcontracting see Appendix.*

Eventually, the Nancy Ann Storybook Doll Company was purchased by Albert M. Bourla and stockholders. In 1966 he requested the help of Fay Redman to instruct very young workers in Hong Kong to cut and sew the costumes for the dolls he was to later present at the Toy Fair in New York in 1967. The dolls were made of plastic, very light in color with a high sheen. His venture lasted only a few years. Many of his dolls were made in Hong Kong.

Just a few years ago an auction of Nancy Ann Storybook plastic doll body parts and accessories from Mr. Bourla's inventory took place. The bulk of this inventory was purchased by one lady in the California area. From these doll parts she has been able to assemble a given doll. She has sewn beautiful outfits for the dolls, trying her best to duplicate the outfits shown in the original advertising brochure listing the plastic Nancy Ann Storybook Dolls. As reported to me by this very talented lady, there were an exceptional number of Muffie heads without bodies to match them. She was able to make a mold for the Muffie body and the name STORYBOOK//DOLLS//CALIFORNIA//MUFFIE appears on the back just as it is marked on the original body. The first Muffies were marked on the back "STORY//BOOK//DOLLS//CALIFORNIA." In no way does she misrepresent the dolls as being the original Nancy Ann Storybook Muffie. However, persons who have purchased the dolls from her have, in turn, resold them as originals. This may not be a problem for those who are familiar with the original Nancy Ann Storybook Muffie dolls, but it does cause problems for those who are not quite familiar with them. The best one can say is "Caveat Emptor" (Buyer Beware).

Illustration 405. Plastic dolls first presented at the New York Toy Fair in 1948 with mohair wigs, jointed arms and legs and movable head (except on the 3½ and 4½in. or 8.9 and 11.4cm versions). They are marked: STORYBOOK DOLLS//U.S.A.//TRADEMARK//REG. Too often all the hard plastic Storybook Dolls with painted features are referred to as composition and often mistaken for bisque.

Illustration 406. Plastic dolls with sleep eyes dating from circa 1950. From left to right: 4½in. (11.4cm) doll with head that does not move, movable arms and legs, white painted boots used as Little Sister (series #50-55) and in a later *Commencement Series* as #71 First Birthday. Next 5½in. (14cm) doll with movable head, arms and legs, white painted gloves and high shoes, used in *Commencement Series* as #73 First Communion. Next, 5½in. (14cm) doll with movable head, arms and legs, slight bust and black painted strapless slippers. Right: 6½in. (16.5cm) doll with movable head, arms and legs, and black painted strapless slippers, used in *Dolls Of The Month Series, Operetta Series* and *All-Time Hit Parade Series*. All are marked: STORY BOOK//DOLLS// U.S.A.//TRADEMARK//REG.

Illustrations 407a and **407b.** Dating from 1950, this 18in. (45.7cm) plastic *Style Doll* (also called "Fashion Doll" by some collectors) has glued on saran wig, sleep eyes, movable head, jointed arms and legs and feet that are flat. There is a very slight bust line and the doll is unmarked. Two buttons were used on some of the outfits just under the material where the bust line should be, to help support the material.

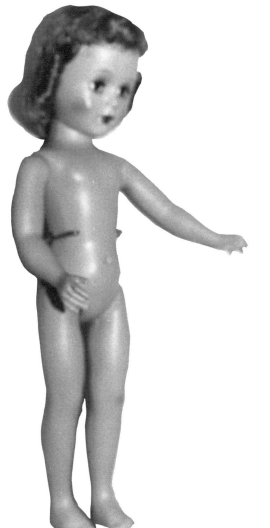

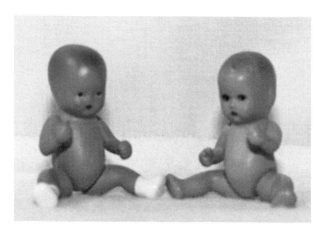

Illustration 408. Both babies are plastic and 3½in. (8.9cm) with jointed arms and legs and closed fists. They are marked on the back: STORY BOOK// DOLLS//U.S.A.// TRADEMARK//REG. Doll on left has painted features, white painted booties and is circa 1948. Doll on right has sleep eyes, molded hair and is circa 1950.

Illustration 409. Doll on left: dating from 1953, 8in. (20.3cm) *Muffie,* all plastic, with dynel wig, sleep eyes, movable head, arms and legs. She is a "walker" in that when her legs move, her head turns from side to side. There is another Muffie with bendable knees not shown. She is marked STORY BOOK // DOLLS // CALIFORNIA//MUFFIE. Right: Reportedly from 1958, 8in. (20.3cm) *Lori Ann* with plastic body and vinyl head with rooted hair, sleep eyes, movable head, arms and legs. She is marked "NANCY ANN" on back of neck.

Illustration 410. Below. Doll on left: Circa 1954 plastic 10in. (25.4cm) *Debbie,* Muffie's big sister, with saran wig, sleep eyes, movable head and arms. She is a straight-leg walker which enables her to turn from side to side when her legs are moved. Right: Another 10in. plastic Debbie with bendable legs and vinyl head with rooted hair. She has jointed arms and legs and sleep eyes. Both dolls are marked on back of neck "NANCY ANN."

Illustration 411a. Below Right. Doll on left: Dating from 1957, 8½in. (21.6cm) *Miss Nancy* with plastic body, vinyl movable head, rooted hair, sleep eyes and jointed arms and legs. Her feet are molded for high-heels. There are no markings. Right: Also from 1957, 10½in. (26.7cm) *Miss Nancy Ann* with plastic body, vinyl movable head, rooted hair, earrings, sleep eyes and movable waist, arms and legs. Her feet are molded for high-heels. She is marked on back of her neck "NANCY ANN."

171

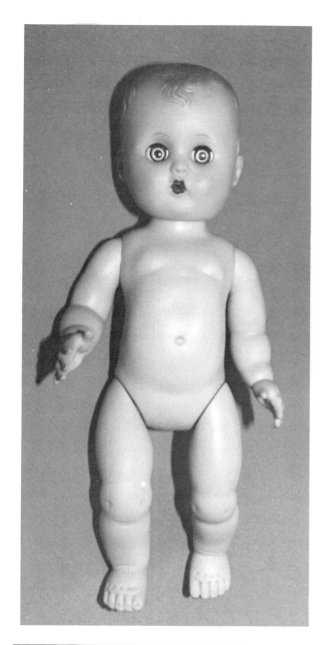

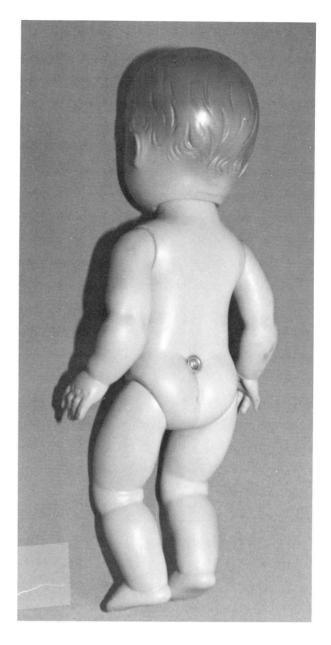

Illustration 411b. Circa late 1950s, 9in. (22.9cm) *Sue Sue,* all vinyl with molded hair, movable head, sleep eyes with lashes, small open nursing mouth, movable arms and legs. She is marked on the back of her neck "NANCY ANN." *Jackie Robertson Collection.*

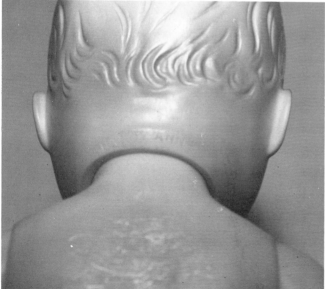

Illustration 411c. Back view of 9in. (22.9cm) vinyl *Sue Sue.* *Jackie Robertson Collection.*

Illustration 411d. 9in. (22.9cm) Vinyl *Sue Sue* showing the "NANCY ANN" marking at the base of her head. *Jackie Robertson Collection.*

Illustration 412. *#401 A Pretty Girl Is Like a Melody:* 6½in. (16.5cm) Plastic with sleep eyes, movable head, arms and legs; blond mohair wig adorned with pink bow and flowers; large off-white horsehair-type hat with large white lace bow at right side. Her pink taffeta bodice is attached to pink underskirt; her overskirt is of white lace with flower design, trimmed with pink satin ribbon around skirt and tied in bow at right side of waist. Flowers are attached to dress and she also wears white pantaloons and black painted strapless slippers.

Illustration 413. *#402. Oh, Suzannah:* 6½in. (16.5cm) Plastic with sleep eyes and jointed arms and legs; movable head; mohair wig; black felt hat with flowers. Doll wears a satin bodice attached to lavender orange-striped skirt, accented by black lace trim. She also wears white pantaloons and black painted strapless slippers. *Marian Schmuhl Collection.*

173

Illustration 414. Above. *#403 Stardust:* 6½in (16.5cm) Plastic with sleep eyes and jointed arms and legs; movable head; dark mohair wig; large horsehair-type hat with lace ribbon, gold cord ties and gold thread interwoven into hat. She wears a long white taffeta dress with gold stripes, trimmed with two rows of white lace sewn to gold cording. She also wears a white underslip with lace trim, white pantaloons and black painted strapless slippers. *Marian Schmuhl Collection.*

Illustration 415. *#405 Jeannie* (also called *Moonlight and Roses*). 6½in. (16.5cm) Plastic with sleep eyes; movable head, arms and legs; blond mohair wig; dark lavender felt hat with gathered net to form bow on top of hat, light lavender ribbon ties and flowers. Doll's bodice is lavender, her overskirt is light lavender graced with white flowers on right side of skirt. Her underskirt is light lavender also, and she wears short white panties and black painted strapless slippers.

Illustration 416. *#406 Only a Rose:* 6½in. (16.5cm) Plastic with sleep eyes; movable head, arms and legs; dark hair; deep pink felt hat covered with white netting and a large pink rose on top. Her long peach satin dress has white lace trim across bodice and an overskirt of white net gathered in center, accented by a large rose and white lace trim. There is also a row of pink trim and white lace around bottom of skirt. She also wears white underskirt, short white panties and black painted strapless slippers.

Illustration 417. *#406. Only a Rose:* 6½in. (16.5cm) Plastic with jointed arms and legs; movable head; sleep eyes; blond mohair wig; white lace hat with white roses. Doll's yellow striped taffeta gown has white lace and white roses. She also wears white underslip, white pantaloons and black painted strapless slippers. *Marian Schmuhl Collection.*

Illustration 418. *#407 Alice Blue Gown:* 6½in. (16.5cm) Plastic with sleep eyes; jointed arms and legs; movable head; blond mohair wig; large blue straw hat with white ribbon bow, flowers and black lace as trim. Doll's bodice is blue and her sleeves are covered in black lace. An overskirt of blue netting with black lace and blue and gold braid trim covers underskirt of blue taffeta. There are flowers at right side of waist with ribbons, white pantaloons and black painted strapless slippers.

Illustration 419. *#407 Alice Blue Gown:* 6½in. (16.5cm) Plastic with jointed arms and legs; movable head; painted eyes; blond mohair wig; blue straw hat with flower and lace trim. She wears a dress of satin with two tiers of lace-like material forming skirt. Doll also has a white underslip, white pantaloons and black painted strapless slippers.

Illustration 420. *#408 Let Me Call You Sweetheart:* 6½in. (16.5cm) Plastic with movable head; painted eyes; jointed arms and legs; auburn mohair wig; large white lace open crown hat with pink ribbon. She wears a pink taffeta bodice and underskirt along with an overskirt of white net and lace. In addition, she has a white underslip, white pantaloons and black painted strapless slippers. *Jackie Robertson Collection.*

Illustration 421. *#409 Over the Rainbow:* 6½in. (16.5cm) Plastic with painted eyes; movable head, arms and legs; blond mohair wig; white gathered netting with open crown and black lace trim attached to pink ribbon tied in bow as headdress. Doll's long pink taffeta dress has gray stripes and gold metallic thread stripes as highlights. There is black lace trim around skirt, and she also wears a white underskirt and black painted strapless slippers.

Illustration 422. Above. *#410 Mary Lou:* 6½in. (16.5cm) Plastic with sleep eyes; dark mohair wig; large net and lace white hat with red ribbon ties. Doll's long white organdy-type dress has small red circular design pattern, lace over top of sleeves, large red flower with white center on right side of waist and red underslip. She also wears black painted strapless slippers. *Norma Csar Collection.*

Illustration 423. *#411 Girl of My Dreams:* 6½in. (16.5cm) Plastic with sleep eyes; movable head, arms and legs; dark hair; large light blue straw hat with lavender ribbon and flowers on top along with lavender ribbon ties. Her long pink taffeta dress has blue velvet cut-out flower sewn to bodice and the same used as trim around skrit. She also wears a white underslip, short panties and black painted strapless slippers.

Illustration 424. Below. *#412 Easter Parade:* 6½in. (16.5cm) Plastic with jointed arms and legs; movable head; painted eyes; blond mohair wig; small flat white felt hat with white net, flower and white ribbon bow. Doll's white satin bodice is attached to full long white net double-layered skirt (lower layer has white large flower design around skirt). Her underslip is of white satin with small lace trim, and she also wears a white bow at waist, white pantaloons and black painted strapless slippers. Her umbrella is made of netting material decorated with flowers and leaves. Notice her original box with white background and blue dots; "Nancy Ann Storybook Dolls" is written between the dots.

Illustration 426. *#70 Christening:* 3½in. (8.9cm) Plastic with sleep eyes; closed fists, jointed arms and legs; molded hair. Doll's long white organdy dress has small lace band around waist, two rows of lace and one row of white satin ribbon around skirt. There are two white satin streamers of ribbon at right side of waist. Doll also wears long white underslip with small lace trim, white diaper and white painted booties.

Illustration 425. Below right. *#412 Easter Parade:* 6½in. (16.5cm) Plastic with sleep eyes; jointed arms and legs; dark mohair wig; large pink straw hat trimmed with black lace, pink ribbon and flowers. Her light yellow flower print nylon-type dress has black lace as trim. She also wears an underslip of yellow taffeta, white pantaloons and her umbrella is of pink taffeta trimmed with black lace and pink flowers.

Illustration 427. *#71 First Birthday:* 4½in. (11.4cm) Plastic with sleep eyes; jointed arms and legs; dark mohair wig; pink fitted hat with pink and blue cording trim plus white feather. Doll's light pink sheer long dress has lace as well as blue and pink cording as trim around skirt and across chest. She also wears a peach satin underslip with small lace trim, diaper and white painted high shoes.

Illustration 428. *#72 First Day of School:* 5½in. (14cm) Plastic with sleep eyes; jointed arms and legs; dark mohair wig; pink felt hat with pink ribbon and cording as trim. She wears a white dress with line design, pink ribbon and silver cord around waist and skirt and white organdy-like underskirt with lace trim. She also wears white painted high shoes. A book with "ABC" is tied to her right wrist.

Illustration 429. *#73 First Communion:* 5½in. (14cm) Plastic with sleep eyes; jointed arms and legs; dark mohair wig; white net trimmed head-dress. Doll wears a three-quarter length satin dress with full white flowered brocaded skirt over an underskirt of white satin with lace trim. She also wears short pantaloons with lace edging, white painted high boots and gloves. A prayer book is tied to right wrist.

Illustration 430. *#74 Graduation:* 6½in. (16.5cm) Plastic with sleep eyes; jointed arms and legs; dark mohair wig; white ribbon tied around hair in bow. Doll's long off-white satin dress has 2in. (5.1cm) wide lace and cording as trim around skirt. She also wears a white cotton slip and panties. There is a white ribbon with diploma attached to her right wrist.

Illustration 431. *#75 Debut:* 6½in. (16.5cm) Plastic with sleep eyes; jointed arms and legs, light mohair wig; large white flower on right side of hair with white ribbon, bow and ribbon trim of silver cording. Doll wears a long white dress in brocade-like flowered print with three rows of silver cording- one at waist and two around skirt. In addition, there are two rows of lace as trim and she also wears a white satin slip, short panties and black painted strapless slippers.

Bridal Series

Illustration 432. *#84 Ring Bearer* and *#85 Flower Girl:* Both dolls are 4½in. (11.4cm) plastics with painted eyes; movable arms and legs; blond mohair wigs. Left: Boy wears pale blue taffeta top that is open in front with white lace trim over sleeves and large ribbon bow at top of shirt. His pants and painted high shoes are also white. Right: Girl wears small white lace headdress with white satin ribbon and pink and blue flowers. Her long white taffeta dress has small rose pattern trimmed with white lace and has an overskirt of white lace accented with pink and blue flowers. She also wears short white panties and white painted high shoes.
NOTE: There are dolls that are bisque to match this pair. Also 5½in. (14cm) Bride and Bridesmaid with the same type of narrow shaped face.

Illustration 433. *#86 Bride* and *#88 Groom:* Both 5½in. (14cm) plastics have sleep eyes; movable head, arms and legs. Left: Girl has dark mohair wig; white net veil with pearl-type crown; long white lace-type dress with white flowers and Bible attached to right wrist; black painted strapless slippers. Right: Boy has short flocked hair with black top hat; white shirt, vest and bow tie; gold chain; black tuxedo with satin trim on lapels and side of trousers; black painted strapless slippers. *Susan Deats Collection.*

Storybook Series

(NOTE: Also called *Mother Goose Series, Fairytale Series, Fairyland Series* and *Nursery Rhyme Series.*)

Illustration 434. *#113 'One—Two' Button My Shoe:* 5½in. (14cm) Plastic with sleep eyes; movable head, arms and legs; auburn mohair wig; light green felt hat with red feather on top and green ribbon streamers in back. Doll wears a three-quarter length black flower print cotton dress with white sleeves and red trim around neck and skirt. She also wears pantaloons and black painted high boots with white dots for buttons.

Illustration 435. *#137 Topsy:* 5½in. (14cm) Plastic with jointed arms and legs; movable head; painted eyes; black mohair wig sewn in center; two red bows on either side of head. Her long polished cotton red and white dress has white lace trim around skirt. She also wears pantaloons and black painted high top shoes with white dots for buttons.

Illustration 436. *#138 Eva:* 5½in. (14cm) Plastic with movable head, arms and legs; painted eyes; blond mohair wig; pink felt hat with white lace trim around hat and pink ribbon ties. Her pink taffeta bodice is attached to pink skirt with flower print; her overskirt is of sheer pink material with one row of white lace around skirt. She also wears pantaloons and black painted strapless slippers.

Illustration 437. *#162 Princess Rosanie:* 5½in. (14cm) Plastic with movable head, arms and legs; painted eyes; blond mohair wig; gold paper crown. Her long taffeta lavender dress has three rows of gold trim and burgundy ribbon is attached to right side of waist with cluster of flowers. She also wears pantaloons and black painted strapless slippers. *Vickie Myers Collection.*

Illustration 438.
#171 Daffy-Down-Dilly:
5½in. (14cm) Plastic with
sleep eyes; jointed arms
and legs; yellow bow and
flower in blond hair. Her
greenish - yellow taffeta
bodice is attached to un-
derskirt, and there is an
overskirt of yellow nylon
with yellow ribbon trim. A
yellow ribbon with yellow
flower graces the right side
of her skirt.

Illustration 439. *#177 See
Saw Marjorie Daw:* 5½in.
(14cm) Plastic with sleep
eyes; movable head, arms
and legs; dark mohair
wig; red felt hat with open
crown, red ribbon ties and
red feather. Doll's long red
taffeta dress has cotton
trim of white with red
flowers and green stems
and leaves around waist
and around skirt. Her
underslip is of stiff white
organdy with blue broken
lines, as are her matching
pantaloons. She also wears
black painted strapless
slippers.

(NOTE: These were also called Birthday Dolls when registered in December 1946; they had been made in bisque since January 1, 1940.)

Illustration 440. Above. *#185 Saturday's Child Must Work for a Living:* 5½in. (14cm) Plastic with painted eyes; movable head, arms and legs; blond hair; white cotton eyelet cap with blue ribbon ties. Doll's dark blue and white checked dress has a white organdy long apron with lace-like trim. She also wears pantaloons of the same material as her dress and black painted strapless slippers.

Illustration 441. *#186 Sunday's Child (The Child That Was Born on the Sabbath Day is Bonny and Blythe and Good and Gay):* 5½in. (14cm) Plastic (matte-type finish which looks like eyes; mohair wig; pink straw hat with flowers. Her dress of white taffeta has pink rosebud design. She also wears pantaloons and black painted strapless slippers. *Marian Schmuhl Collection.*

Dolls
of the Month
Series

Illustration 442. #189 A Breezy Girl and Arch to Worship Me Through March: 6½in. (16.5cm) Plastic with painted eyes; jointed arms and legs and swivel head; dark mohair; blue felt hat with open crown and streamers and bows of yellow and pink. Doll wears a long taffeta striped dress (yellow-blue-pink-lavender) accented by streamers of pink and yellow ribbon at right side of waist and yellow lace trim around skirt. She also wears white underslip, pantaloons and black painted strapless slippers.

Illustration 443. #191 A Flower Girl for May: 6½in. (16.5cm) Plastic with movable head, arms and legs; painted eyes; blond mohair wig; large pink felt hat with pink bow in back. Doll wears a pink nylon rose print dress with pink ribbon streamers on right side of waist, a pink taffeta under-skirt, white pantaloons and black painted strapless slippers.

Illustration 444. *#195 September's Girl Is Like a Storm:* 6½in. (16.5cm) Plastic with sleep eyes; movable head, arms and legs; auburn mohair wig; light blue circular felt hat with lavender feather and bow on top. Doll's beige bodice is attached to lavender taffeta underskirt; her overskirt is of sheer blue with white embossed small flower design There are two shades of lavender ribbons and bows at right side of waist and white lace trim around skirt. She also wears white pantaloons and black painted strapless slippers.

Illustration 445. *#196 A Sweet October Maiden Rather Shy:* 6½in. (16.5cm) Plastic with painted eyes; movable head and jointed arms and legs; blond mohair wig; circular flat felt hat of deep pink with light lavender bow on top, sewn to lavender ribbon around hair with large bow on right side. Doll's long deep pink taffeta dress has one row of lavender ribbon around skirt and bow with streamers on right side of waist. She also wears white underslip, pantaloons and black painted strapless slippers.

Illustration 446. *#197 A November Lass to Cheer:* 6½in. (16.5cm) Plastic with painted features; movable head; jointed arms and legs; blond mohair wig; pink felt bonnet with lace trim and pink flowers. Her dress is a dark blue taffeta gown with a length of white lace adorned with flowers sewn at waist extending to hem. She also wears white slip, pantaloons and black painted strapless slippers. *Marian Schmuhl Collection.*

Illustration 447. Below. *#198 For December Just a Dear (Oh,I Want a Girl for Each Month of the Year):*6½in. (16.5cm) Plastic with painted eyes; movable head, arms and legs; red mohair wig; red fitted felt hat with red feather and ribbon ties. Her long dark green taffeta dress has wide lace trim, large red ribbon bows and red berries. She also wears white underslip, pantaloons and black painted strapless slippers.

189

Illustration 448. *#302 Dolly Varden:* 6½in. (16.5cm) Plastic with movable head, arms and legs; sleep eyes; blond mohair wig with cluster of pink and blue flowers; large blue straw hat with pink ribbon ties. She wears a long pink taffeta dress with rose print, trimmed in blue lace at bodice (either row extends over shoulders and down back) and around skirt. She also wears a long net underslip, pink taffeta pantaloons and black painted strapless slippers.

Operette Series

Illustration 450. *#306 Fortune Teller:* 6½in. (16.5cm) Plastic with painted eyes; movable head, arms and legs; dark mohair wig; large gold wire band attached to wide red satin ribbon to form hat. Doll's lavender taffeta bodice is accented by white net sleeves and taffeta circular striped (pink-green-orange-yellow-rose-light and dark blue) long skirt with wide red ribbon streamers at right side of waist. She also wears pantaloons and black painted strapless slippers. *Jackie Robertson Collection.*

Illustration 449. *#305 New Moon:* 6½in. (16.5cm) Plastic with painted eyes; jointed arms and legs; auburn mohair wig; small pink band around head with clusters of flowers on each side. Her peach cape is trimmed with pink cord and she wears a long white taffeta dress with vee-shaped cord trim on bodice. The dress also has large lace sleeves, three rows of pink cording around skirt and the doll wears white underslip, white pantaloons and black painted strapless slippers. *Lenore Lev Collection.*

Illustration 451. *#308 My Maryland:* 6½in. (16.5cm) Plastic with jointed arms and legs; painted eyes; large felt hat with black lace and flower decoration on top and ribbon ties. Her long taffeta dress is a black circular striped pattern with pink ribbon trim around skirt and a cluster of flowers on right side near ribbon. There is also black lace trim beneath the pink ribbon, and she wears pantaloons and black painted strapless slippers. *Norma Csar Collection.*

Illustration 452. *#309 Red Mill:* 6½in. (16.5cm) Plastic with sleep eyes; movable head, arms and legs; blond mohair wig; white organdy Dutch-type hat with red ribbon and bow in back. Her long green and white striped taffeta dress has red tulip and green leaf trim around waist and across edge of white organdy apron. There is also one row of red ribbon trim around skirt and she also wears pantaloons and black painted strapless slippers. *Jackie Robertson Collection.*

Religious Series

Illustration 453. *#80 Nun* (Black Habit): 5½in. (14cm) Plastic with movable head, arms and legs. Along with her black habit, which has a black cord around waist with silver cross attached, she wears a black underskirt, black pantaloons and black painted high top shoes.

Illustration 454. *#81 Nun* (White and Black Habit): 5½in. (14cm) Plastic with sleep eyes; movable head, arms and legs. She wears her black habit which has a black cord around waist with silver cross attached, along with white underslip, pantaloons and black painted high shoes. *Susan Deats Collection.*

Illustration 455. *Dale Evans and Roy Rogers:* Left: 8in. (20.3cm) plastic doll; sleep eyes; movable head, arms and legs; dark synthetic wig; large white felt hat; yellow short ribbon as ties around neck. Her shirt is cotton red plaid; belt and holsters are brown with two small silver-colored guns. Doll's skirt is light brown suede with three small gold rivets down center of shirt. Her boots are brown felt with yellow design, and her white panties have lace trim. Right: 8in. (20.3cm) Plastic doll; sleep eyes; movable head, arms and legs; painted light brown hair; large white felt cowboy hat; yellow ribbon tied around neck. He wears a cotton plaid shirt and two brown leather belts—one holding two holsters with small silver guns. His blue jeans are covered with chaps made of light brown suede and there are small gold rivets along sides. His dark brown felt boots also have yellow design. (NOTE: Each of the above dolls have flat-feet. Boxes used for these dolls depart from those we have been accustomed to (with the various colored dots)—instead, a western scene is featured. Circa 1955.) *Photo by Dale Gathman.*

Valentine Sweetheart

Illustration 456. *Sweetheart* (This doll has no number): 5½in. (14cm) Plastic with sleep eyes; movable head; arms and legs; auburn mohair wig; large red felt hat with open crown, red ribbon ties and bow. Doll's three-quarter length dress has bodice of red taffeta and skirt of sheer material with red and white hearts and one row of red ribbon and one row of white lace as trim. She also wears red taffeta panties and black painted strapless slippers.

Big Sister Series

Illustration 457. *#63 Big Sister Goes Shopping:* 5½in. (14cm) plastic with sleep eyes; movable head, arms and legs; blond hair pulled back and tied with red ribbon. She wears a short red and white checked dress with lace trim at shoulders and other trim across chest and around skirt. She also wears short white panties and white painted boots. (NOTE: Some #63 Big Sister dolls are referred to as "Big Sister Goes to Dancing School.")

Muffie

Illustration 458a. 8in. (20.3cm) Plastic Muffie appeared on the back of one of Nancy Ann Storybook Dolls' business cards.

STORYBOOK   MISS NANCY ANN   MUFFIE

NANCY ANN *Storybook* DOLLS, INC.

Manufacturers of the Original 'Storybook Dolls'

1262 POST
SAN FRANCISCO 9, CALIF.
ORDWAY 3-8050

DEBBIE   LET'S PRETEND COSTUMES   SUE SUE

Illustration 458b. One of the company's business cards which pictured Muffie on the reverse side.

Illustration 459. Muffie's Pal with body made of wool felt that has been stuffed and stitched and measures 2½in. high by 3in. long (6.4 x 7.6cm). The dog's legs were made from fuzzy pipe cleaners and the price was originally $1.25. *Kathy Amick Collection.*

195

A LETTER TO NEW PLAYMATE:

If you look like this or maybe like this or even like Muffie herself or best of all if you look just like yourself...

Then you and Muffie are sure to have fun being playmates together!

Would you like to know how Muffie came to be? Turn this page real quick and I'll tell you

ACCESSORIES

(Top row—l. to r.)				(Bottom row—l. to r.)	
915X Roller Skates	.50	919X Glasses (4)	1.00	923X Clothes Hangers .25	926X Genuine Mink Muff 1.00
916X Shoes & Socks	.50	920X Suit Case	1.00	924X Separate Wig 1.00	927X Can-Can Petticoats (2) 1.00
917X Ice Skates	.50	921X Straw Hat	.79	925X Poodle Dog 1.25	
918X Plastic Raincoat 1.00		922X Doll Stand	.25		

Illustrations 460a, b, c, d, e and f: Original advertising for Muffie which shows the many outfits and accessories available for her.

WARDROBE SETS

957 Wardrobe Chest   5.98
Includes Muffie with shoes, socks, 2 dresses, hat and other accessories.

958 Wardrobe Trunk   13.98
Includes Muffie with night gown and slippers, red sleeper, 2 dresses, coat and hat, extra shoes and socks and other accessories.

the sweetest dolls this side of heaven!

NANCY ANN *Storybook* DOLLS, INC.

1262 Post Street • San Francisco 9, California

Illustration 460a.

HOW MUFFIE CAME TO BE

Once upon a time, not too long ago when I was a little girl just like you, I played with a Muffie but my Muffie was only make-believe, not a real doll Muffie at all.

Then one day I thought what fun it would be to have a real Muffie for a playmate—a cute little doll playmate just big enough to carry in my pocket, or in my bicycle basket, to go to a friend's house to play, and even to school with me!

She'd have her own shoes and purses and hats (these are called "accessories"), and of course, she'd have lots of pretty dresses and coats and costumes, just as many as I did so that she could do everything we wanted to do together.

She would have her own trunk and suitcase so she could go traveling with me, and even special Muffie-size chairs and a table and her own little bed and a wardrobe to keep her clothes in.

That's how Muffie came to be. And if you look at all the pretty pictures of Muffie in this letter, you can choose the things you'd like to have for your own Muffie.

Your friend,   Nancy Ann

Nancy Ann

GAY COTTON PRINTS

501 Dressed Doll 3.29	503 Dressed Doll 3.29	505 Dressed Doll 3.29	507 Dressed Doll 3.29
501X Outfit Only 1.60	503X Outfit Only 1.60	505X Outfit Only 1.60	507X Outfit Only 1.60
502 Dressed Doll 3.29	504 Dressed Doll 3.29	506 Dressed Doll 3.29	508 Dressed Doll 3.29
502X Outfit Only 1.60	504X Outfit Only 1.60	506X Outfit Only 1.60	508X Outfit Only 1.60

FAVORITE FASHIONS

601 Dressed Doll 3.59	603 Dressed Doll 3.59	605 Dressed Doll 3.59	607 Dressed Doll 3.59
601X Outfit Only 1.98	603X Outfit Only 1.98	605X Outfit Only 1.98	607X Outfit Only 1.98
602 Dressed Doll 3.59	604 Dressed Doll 3.59	606 Dressed Doll 3.59	608 Dressed Doll 3.59
602X Outfit Only 1.98	604X Outfit Only 1.98	606X Outfit Only 1.98	608X Outfit Only 1.98

PINAFORE STYLES

652 Dressed Doll 3.59	654 Dressed Doll 3.59	656 Dressed Doll 3.59	658 Dressed Doll 3.59
652X Outfit Only 1.98	654X Outfit Only 1.98	656X Outfit Only 1.98	658X Outfit Doll 1.98
651 Dressed Doll 3.59	653 Dressed Doll 3.59	655 Dressed Doll 3.59	657 Dressed Doll 3.59
651X Outfit Only 1.98	653X Outfit Only 1.98	655X Outfit Only 1.98	657X Outfit Only 1.98

Illustration 460b.

DRESS-UP STYLES

701 Dressed Doll 4.29   703 Dressed Doll 4.29   705 Dressed Doll 4.29   707 Dressed Doll 4.29
701X Outfit Only 2.50   703X Outfit Only 2.50   705X Outfit Only 2.50   707X Outfit Only 2.50

702 Dressed Doll 4.29   704 Dressed Doll 4.29   706 Dressed Doll 4.29   708 Dressed Doll 4.29
702X Outfit Only 2.50   704X Outfit Only 2.50   706X Outfit Only 2.50   708X Outfit Only 2.50

SPECIAL OCCASION STYLES

802 Dressed Doll 3.59   804 Dressed Doll 4.29   806 Dressed Doll 4.29   808 Dressed Doll 4.29
802X Outfit Only 1.98   804X Outfit Only 2.50   806X Outfit Only 2.50   808X Outfit Only 2.50

801 Dressed Doll 3.59   803 Dressed Doll 3.59   805 Dressed Doll 4.29   807 Dressed Doll 4.29
801X Outfit Only 1.98   803X Outfit Only 1.98   805X Outfit Only 2.50   807X Outfit Only 2.50

SPECIAL OCCASION STYLES

810 Dressed Doll 4.75   812 Dressed Doll 5.98
810X Outfit Only 2.98   812X Coat & Hat Only 2.98

809 Dressed Doll 4.75   811 Dressed Doll 4.75
809X Outfit Only 2.98   811X Outfit Only 2.98   White   Leopard

#500B
plastic head
Saran wig
bending knees
1.98

#500C
vinyl head
rooted Saran hair
straight legs
1.98

#500D
vinyl head
rooted Saran hair
bending knees
2.49

#500
plastic head
Saran wig
straight legs
1.59

UNDRESSED MUFFIES
with plastic shoes, socks and lace trimmed panties

Illustration 460c.

198

BRIDAL PARTY

900 Dressed Doll 5.29
(only)

901 Dressed Doll 5.29
901X Outfit Only 3.50

902 Dressed Doll 5.29
902X Outfit Only 3.50

902 Dressed Doll 5.29
902X Outfit Only 3.50

SPECIAL OCCASION STYLES

903 Dressed Doll 4.50
903X Outfit Only 2.98

905 Dressed Doll 3.59
905X Outfit Only 1.98

907 Dressed Doll 3.59
907X Outfit Only 1.98

909 Dressed Doll 3.59
909X Outfit Only 1.98

904 Dressed Doll 3.29
904X Outfit Only 1.60

906 Dressed Doll 3.59
906X Outfit Only 1.98

908 Dressed Doll 3.59
908X Outfit Only 1.98

SPECIAL OCCASION STYLES

910 Dressed Doll 3.59
910X Outfit Only 1.98

912 Dressed Doll 3.59
912X Outfit Only 1.98

914 Dressed Doll 3.59
914X Outfit Only 1.98

911 Dressed Doll 3.59
911X Outfit Only 1.98

913 Dressed Doll 3.29
913X Outfit Only 1.60

SPECIAL OCCASION STYLES

951 Dressed Doll 9.98
951X Dress Only 3.98

953 Dressed Doll 10.98
953X Dress Only 3.98

952 Dressed Doll 10.98
952X Dress Only 3.98

954 Dressed Doll 11.98
954X Dress Only 3.98

Illustration 460d.

199

Illustration 460e.

muffie's special occasion styles

THEY WALK!

801   802   803   804   805   806   807   808

muffie's special occasion styles

THEY WALK!

809   810   811   812   901   902   903

WARDROBE chest and trunk

THEY WALK!

907   908

muffie's separate accessories

THEY WALK!

915 916 917 918 919   920   921   Undressed Muffie with some of her wardrobes

Illustration 460f.

Debbie

Illustration 461a. Debbie (Muffie's Big Sister): 10in. (25.4cm) Plastic with glued on wig and straight legs. Her white satin bridal dress has white lace trim and her white net veil has a stiff crown. There are large white flowers with white satin ribbon on right side of waist and she also wears a long taffeta underslip, short panties and metallic strapless shoes. *Marge Meisinger Collection.*

Illustration 461b. Debbie (Muffie's Big Sister): 10in. (25.4cm) Plastic with glued on wig. She wears a dark blue cotton coat with white organdy collar over a blue and white checked dress. Her tam is of white organdy with a pink band she wears white panties, red socks and dark blue shoes. *Marge Meisinger Collection.*

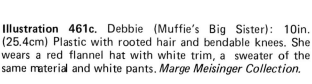

Illustration 461c. Debbie (Muffie's Big Sister): 10in. (25.4cm) Plastic with rooted hair and bendable knees. She wears a red flannel hat with white trim, a sweater of the same material and white pants. *Marge Meisinger Collection.*

Illustration 462. *Miss Nancy Ann:* 10½in. (26.7cm) vinyl head with mature plastic body; movable head and waist; rooted dark hair; red hat. Doll is dressed in a pink plain dress with white trim around collar and lace trim around three-quarter length sleeves. Her underclothing consists of a lace bra and panties. She also wears black high-heeled shoes with straps.

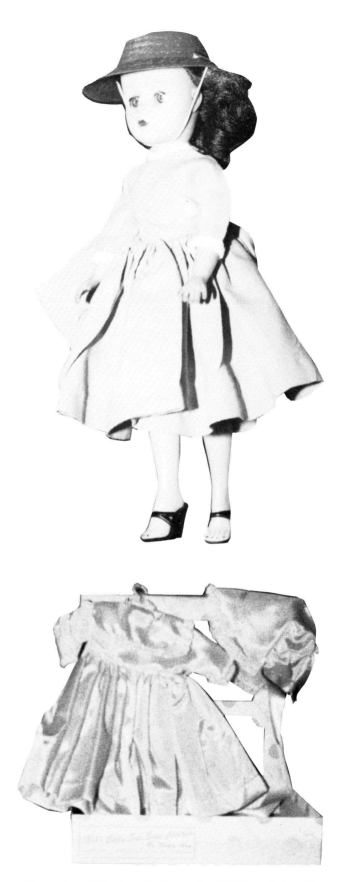

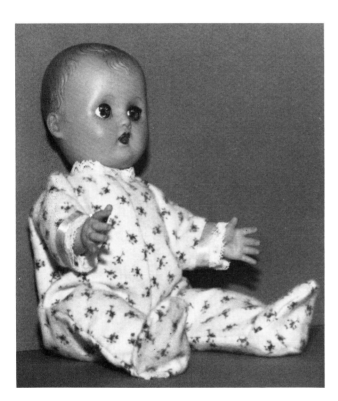

Illustration 463. *Sue Sue:* 9in. (22.5cm) All vinyl baby doll with molded hair; large sleep eyes with lashes; painted eyebrows; open mouth. She is wearing white flannel with red rosebud print pajamas, trimmed with pink ribbon and white lace around sleeves. There is also white lace trim around collar and matching diaper with snaps on each side. The clothing is marked "by Nancy Ann, San Francisco, California." Doll is marked "Nancy Ann" on back of neck. *Jackie Robertson Collection.*

Illustration 464. *Sue Sue's outfit #1011x:* Pink taffeta dress with white lace trim; bonnet also of pink taffeta with lace trim and ribbon ties. A pink diaper also came with this set. *Marge Meisinger Collection.*

203

Style Doll

Illustration 465. *#1901 Tea Roses:* 18in. (45.7cm) All-plastic *Style Doll* with saran wig; small straw hat with flowers and wide satin ribbon ties. Her long blue lace dress has a flower pattern, and the lining is of pink taffeta. Her underslip has hoop at edge and she wears nylon hose with flat satin slippers.

Illustration 466. *#2403 Lemon Frost:* 18in. (45.7cm) All plastic *Style Doll* with saran wig; large straw hat with yellow velvet flowers. Doll wears a long light yellow dress of nylon with yellow stripes and yellow velvet ribbon around waist and skirt as trim. Her light yellow underslip is of taffeta with a hoop at edge. She also wears nylon hose and gold slippers.

1503

Enchantment

$15.95
retail price

Actual Size of Dolls

Style
Show
by
Nancy Ann

Illustration 467 a, b, c and d: Samples of original advertising for the *Style Dolls,* also referred to as dolls from *Style Show Series.*

Style Show
by Nancy Ann

CREATOR OF 'STORYBOOK DOLLS'

Nancy Ann presents her new 18" Plastic Dolls with Saran Wigs.

Each doll is exquisite in individually designed gowns of woven taffetas, silk, nylon and embroidered nets and imported French laces. Trimmings include sequins, nosegays of flowers and ribbons. Some of the dolls have flower and ribbon-trimmed straw hats. Each doll wears a hooped petticoat under a very full skirt, which gives a beautiful bouffant appearance. Full fashioned nylon net hose with satin or gold slippers complete the ensemble.

All dresses have snaps and are removable. The saran wigs are individually styled. To choose from are upswept hairdos, pony tails, page boy coiffures and hairdos of curls and swirls, in assorted colors to complement the gowns.

NANCY ANN STORYBOOK DOLLS, INC. · 1298 POST STREET · SAN FRANCISCO 9, CALIFORNIA

1501 Summery Day $15.95	1502 Breath of Spring $15.95
1504 Lilac Time $15.95	1901 Afternoon Tea $19.95
1902 Heavenly Blue $19.95	1903 Demure Miss $19.95	1904 Garden Party $19.95
2401 Moonlight Mist $24.95	2402 Dinner Date $24.95	2403 Sweet and Lovely $24.95
2404 Sophistication $24.95	2901 Grand Bal $29.95	2902 Gay Evening $29.95
2903 Opera Night $29.95	2904 Wedding Day $29.95	3401 Her Royal Majesty Wedding $34.95

Illustration 467b.

style show series

1501 Miss Checker Board   THEY WALK!   1502 Pinkie

style show series

1503 White Lilacs   THEY WALK!   1504 Strawberry Festival

style show series

1901 Miss Pinafore   THEY WALK!   1902 Golden Gleam

style show series

1903 Summer Afternoon   THEY WALK!   1904 Sweet Miss

Illustration 467c.

207

style show series

2401 Gaiety   THEY WALK!   2402 Pink Pearl

style show series

2403 Senior Prom   THEY WALK!   2404 Lace Butterflies

style show series

2901 Beautiful Lady THEY WALK!   2902 Forget-me-not

style show series

2903 Dinner Dance   THEY WALK!   2904 Bride

Illustration 467d.

208

VI. Nancy Ann Furniture Patterns

(Note: A copy of the original McCall Pattern circa 1940).

GENERAL DIRECTIONS

TO CUT— All seams are allowed on pattern pieces except patterns for cardboard foundation. Use light weight flexible cardboard. Do *not* cut the notches in cardboard. All cardboard foundation pieces must be completely covered with material. To do this, place cardboard on material, allowing 1/4in. (6.35mm) extra for seams around entire edge of each piece. Mark around all cardboard edges with pencil and cut 1/4in. (6.35mm) beyond pencil marks.

TO COVER CARDBOARD — Join material for each section (sewing along the pencil line) leaving one edge free to insert cardboard. Turn right side out and press, then insert cardboard, turn in seam allowance of opening and slipstitch edges together.

After covering each cardboard section, join edges of sections together as notched using small whipping stitches and matching thread.

TO STUFF OR PAD — Use cotton batting or floss.

BASSINET (A) — Cover all cardboard foundation sections in blue except the pad foundation (see general directions.) Join side section to front and back, then join to bottom.
- Gather upper and lower edges of inside facing along lines indicated.
- Arrange facing on inside of bassinet, bringing the top gathered edge over the bassinet about 1/2in. (12.7mm) and sew. Sew lower edge to position.

FOR HOOD — Make narrow hem at front edge and trim with ribbon 3/8in. (9.53mm) wide. Sew together on lines indicated to form small tucks. Insert wire through tucks and bend ends of wire at right angles for 1/2in. (12.7mm). Gather back edge of hood, and sew to position on bassinet so that circles on hood will match corners of bassinet.

McCALL

PRINTED PATTERN

811

Pattern for Doll Furniture
For Dolls 4 to
7 Inches High.
(10.2 to 17.8cm)

Bassinett for Smaller Dolls
Bed 5 x 8 Inches
(12.7 x 20.3cm)

illustration by Linda K. David

FOR RUFFLE — Join ends, turn up lower edge on right side of material and stitch. Sew ribbon to position on line indicated. Turn under upper edge and gather. Sew ruffle to bassinet along the gathering line. Trim with pink and blue ribbons 9in. (22.9cm) long tied in a bow.

FOR PAD — Join seams of material for slipcover, leaving one end open. Overcast edges of cotton batting to one side of cardboard foundation. Insert padded cardboard into slipcover and close opening.

FOR PILLOW — Place white material over blue lining, join seams, turn right side out and stuff.

FOR COVER — Place white material over blue lining and pink the edges. Tie small pink and blue ribbon bows and tack the 2 bows to center of cover sewing through lining.

DRESSING TABLE (B) - Cover cardboard foundation sections (see general directions). Then join back to front. Join table top to back and front in same manner.
● Finish side and lower edges of skirt with hems, then turn under upper edge and gather, drawing gathers into 10-1/2in. (26.3cm). Sew skirt to table edge, trim with 3/8in. (9.53mm) wide ribbon and bow.
● Attach mirror as follows: Cut a piece of cardboard 3in. (7.6cm) long plus the height of mirror and about the same width as mirror. Cover cardboard with material and paste to back of mirror and table.

DRESSING TABLE STOOL (C) — Cover cardboard side foundation (see general directions). Pad cardboard stool top foundation. Cover smaller circle with material, one side only. Place both circles together onto material circle, gather around edge and pull together tightly to fit snug. Whip ends of covered side section together and join to top.
● Join ends of ruffle, make hem at lower edge, gather upper edge and sew to stool. Sew ribbon to edge of top and trim with bow.

CHAIR (D) — Pad upper part of cardboard side sections on inside with cotton batting and cover all cardboard foundation sections. (See general directions). Joint front to seat section, then join side to back and front. Sew seat to chair underneath seat.

FOR RUFFLE — Make hem at lower edge of ruffle, join ends, turn under upper edge and gather on lines indicated and draw in gathering to fit entire edge of chair. Sew ruffle to chair (lower edges even). Make cushions and stuff.

OTTOMAN (E) — Cover all cardboard foundation sections (see general directions). Join the four side sections, then join to seat section. Make ruffle and sew to ottoman in same manner as chair. Make cushion and stuff.

SOFA (F) — Pad upper part of cardboard side sections on inside with cotton batting and cover all cardboard foundation sections (see general directions). Join front and inner back to seat.
● Join side sections to outer back and front. Sew inner back to outer back 1/2in. (12.7mm) above lower edge.
● Make ruffle and finish sofa in same manner as chair (D).

BED (G) — Join the two sections of material for back together leaving lower edge free. Overcast edges of cotton batting to position on one side of cardboard foundation, then insert foundation into slipcover and close opening.
● Tuft padded section of back using one strand pearl cotton No. 3 and heavy needle. Pull thread through all thicknesses of material and cardboard taking a small stitch, tying thread in tight double knot on padded side and clipping ends of thread. Make tufts about 1in. (2.5cm) apart. Make front in same manner. Cover remaining cardboard foundation pieces according to general directions.
● Join side sections to inner back and inner front sections, then join to bed sections. Arrange front (padded side turned out) over inner front, lower edges even and whip together, then sew together across lower edge of padding.
● Join back (padded side truned in) to inner back in same manner.
● Make ruffle and sew to bed in same manner as chair (D).

MATTRESS — Join ends of side band, then join between the top and lower section of mattress to form boxing, leaving one edge open. Cut a piece of cotton batting 5-1/4 x 8-1/4in. (13.1 x 20.6cm) and 1/2in. (12.7mm) thick. Insert batting and close seam. Form 1/8in. (3.17mm) tuck along seams of boxing and stitch. Then tuft mattress as indicated by dots given on pattern.

PILLOW — Join seams of pillow and stuff.

WHITE PILLOW CASE — Make hem and join seams.

WHITE SHEET — Make hems as indicated.

COLORED BLANKET — Pink entire outer edge.

BEDSPREAD AND SHAM — Trim with bands of folded bias binding tape No. 5. Pink outer edges of bedspread and sham. Then join seam of sham.

ASSEMBLING, SEWING AND FINISHING DETAILS

Join the seams by matching the corresponding notches. The notches in the pattern are numbered in the order in which the seams should be joined.

For all pieces of furniture, cover cardboard foundation sections with chosen material according to general directions.

BASSINET A.

- Notches 1 to 5. Join seams, matching notches, and make bassinet according to general directions.
- Make pad, pillow and cover according to general directions.

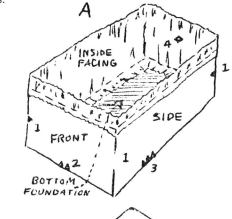

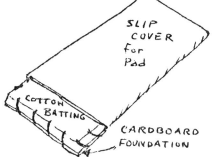

HOOD

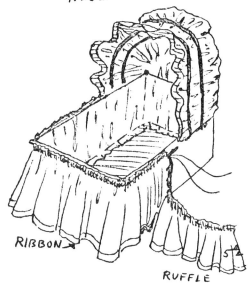

BASSINET

RIBBON

RUFFLE

DRESSING TABLE B.

- Join front and side to back; then to top (see general directions).
- Make skirt, sew to table and fasten to back according to general directions.

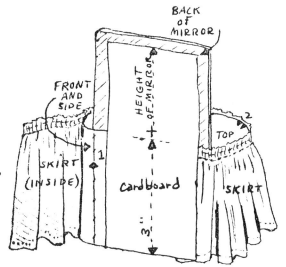

DRESSING TABLE B

STOOL C.

- Join seam of side and join to padded top (see general directions.
- Join seam of ruffle and hem lower edge; then sew gathered edge to stool and trim with ribbon (see general directions).

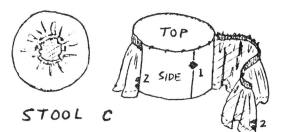

STOOL C

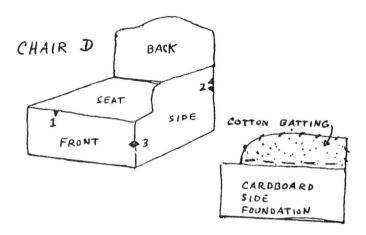

CHAIR D

CHAIR D.
- Pad side foundation to line indicated; then cover all foundation pieces (see general directions).
- Join front to seat; then join side to front and back.
- Join seat to position on back and sides beneath the chair. Ruffles and cushions, (see general directions).

SOFA F.
- Sew seat to front and inner back.
- Pad side sections to line indicated and cover with material.
- Join side sections to outer back.
- Join sides to front.
- Sew inner back to outer back 1/2in. (12.7mm) above lower edge. Make ruffle and finish sofa in same manner as chair D.

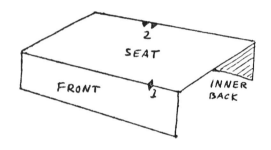

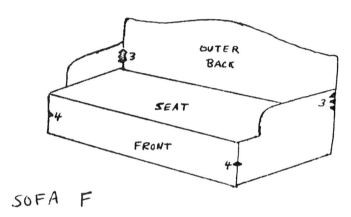

SOFA F

BED G.
- Tuft front and back according to general directions.
- Sew sides to inner front and inner back; then join to bed section.
- Finish bed cording to general directions.
- Join ends of side band; then sew to mattress.
- Finish mattress, etc. according to general directions.

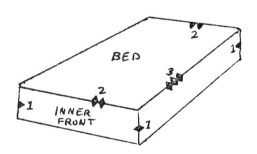

BED G

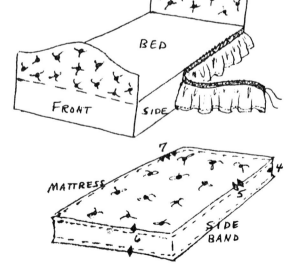

OTTOMAN E.
- See general directions.

BASSINET A

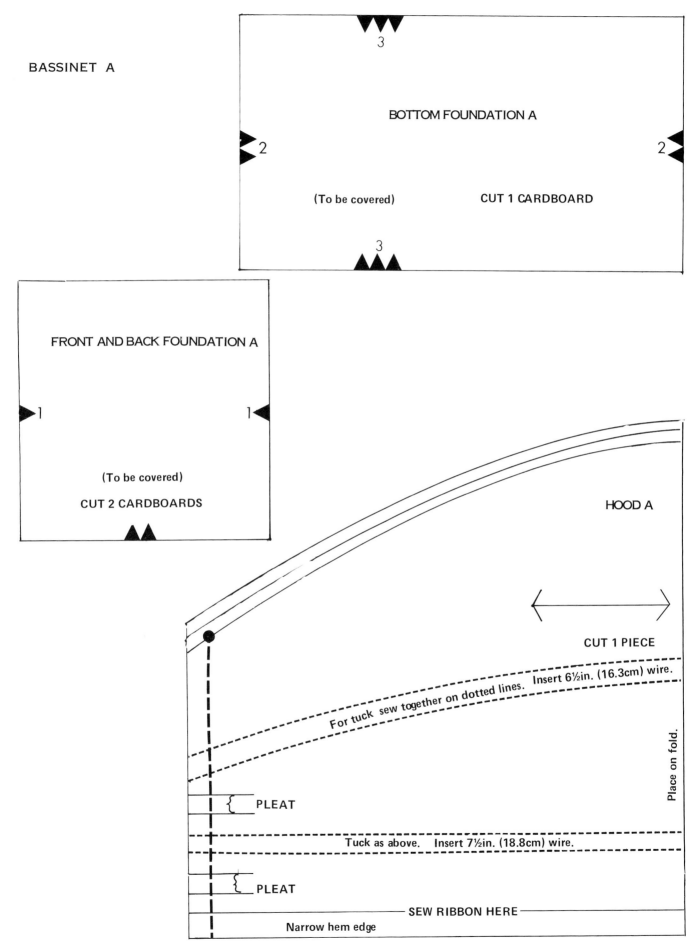

BOTTOM FOUNDATION A

3

2   2

(To be covered)   CUT 1 CARDBOARD

3

FRONT AND BACK FOUNDATION A

1   1

(To be covered)

CUT 2 CARDBOARDS

HOOD A

CUT 1 PIECE

For tuck sew together on dotted lines.   Insert 6½in. (16.3cm) wire.

Place on fold.

} PLEAT

Tuck as above.   Insert 7½in. (18.8cm) wire.

} PLEAT

SEW RIBBON HERE

Narrow hem edge

213

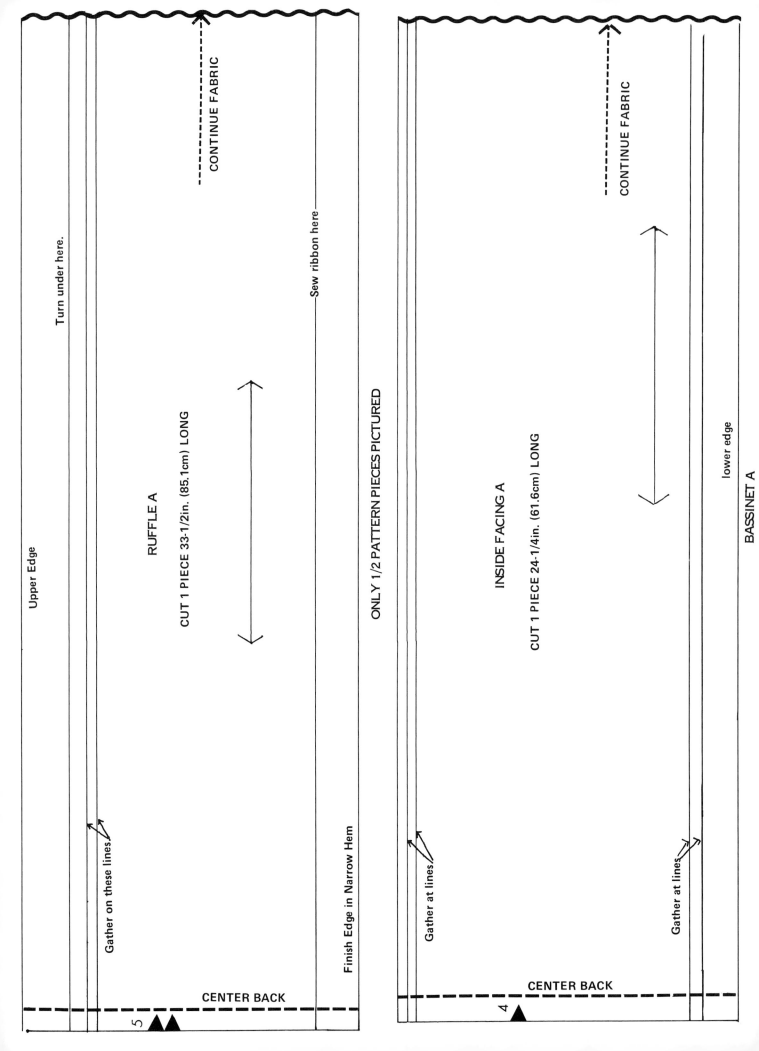

CONTINUE FABRIC

Turn under here.

Upper Edge

RUFFLE A

CUT 1 PIECE 33-1/2in. (85.1cm) LONG

Sew ribbon here

Gather on these lines

Finish Edge in Narrow Hem

CENTER BACK

5

ONLY 1/2 PATTERN PIECES PICTURED

CONTINUE FABRIC

INSIDE FACING A

CUT 1 PIECE 24-1/4in. (61.6cm) LONG

Gather at lines

Gather at lines

lower edge

BASSINET A

CENTER BACK

4

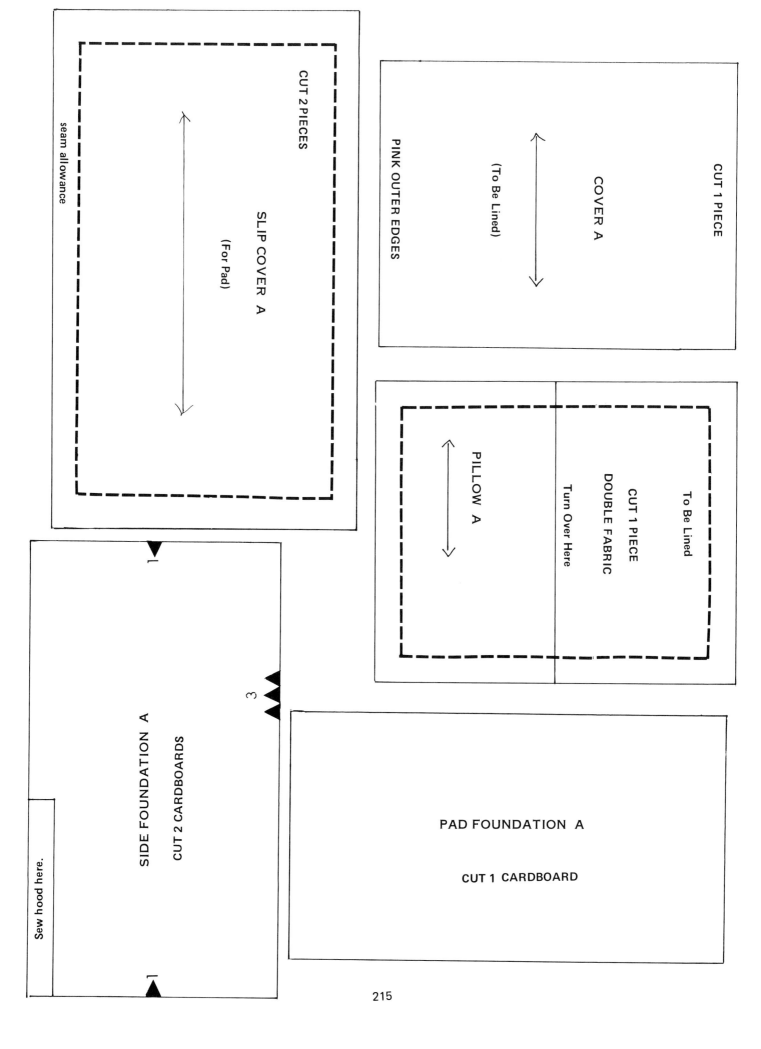

CUT 2 PIECES

SLIP COVER A

(For Pad)

seam allowance

CUT 1 PIECE

PINK OUTER EDGES

COVER A

(To Be Lined)

CUT 1 PIECE
DOUBLE FABRIC

Turn Over Here

To Be Lined

PILLOW A

SIDE FOUNDATION A

CUT 2 CARDBOARDS

3

1

1

Sew hood here.

PAD FOUNDATION A

CUT 1 CARDBOARD

215

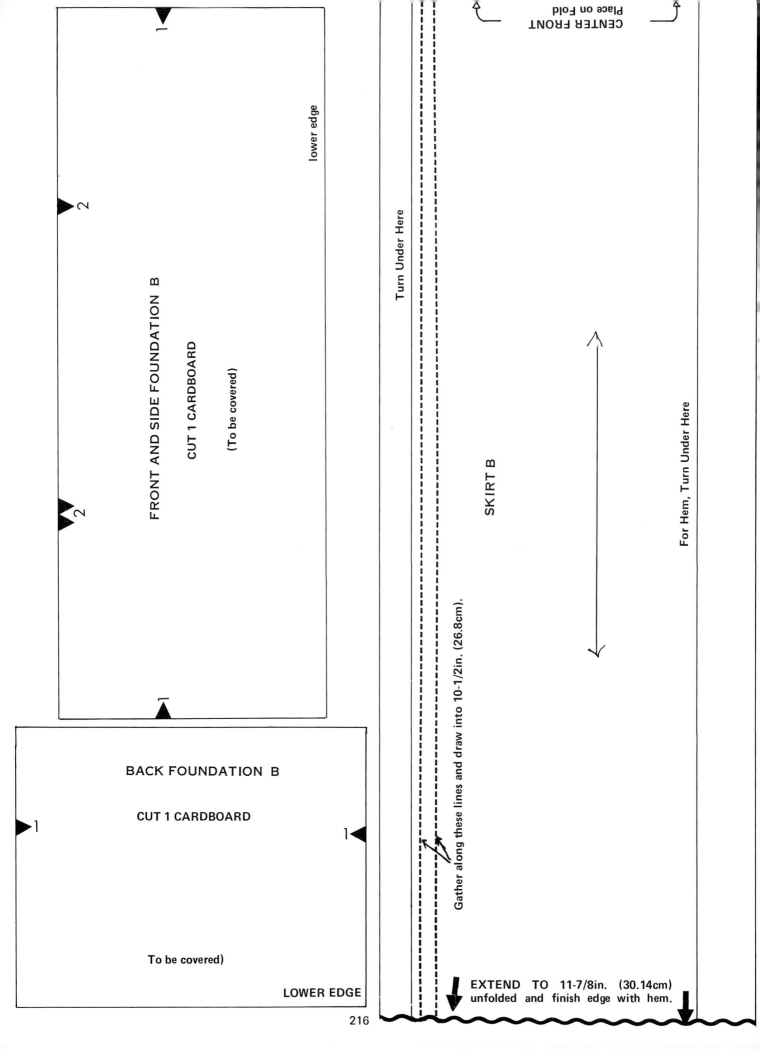

FRONT AND SIDE FOUNDATION B

CUT 1 CARDBOARD

(To be covered)

lower edge

BACK FOUNDATION B

CUT 1 CARDBOARD

To be covered)

LOWER EDGE

CENTER FRONT
Place on Fold

Turn Under Here

SKIRT B

For Hem, Turn Under Here

Place on Fold

Gather along these lines and draw into 10-1/2in. (26.8cm).

EXTEND TO 11-7/8in. (30.14cm)
unfolded and finish edge with hem.

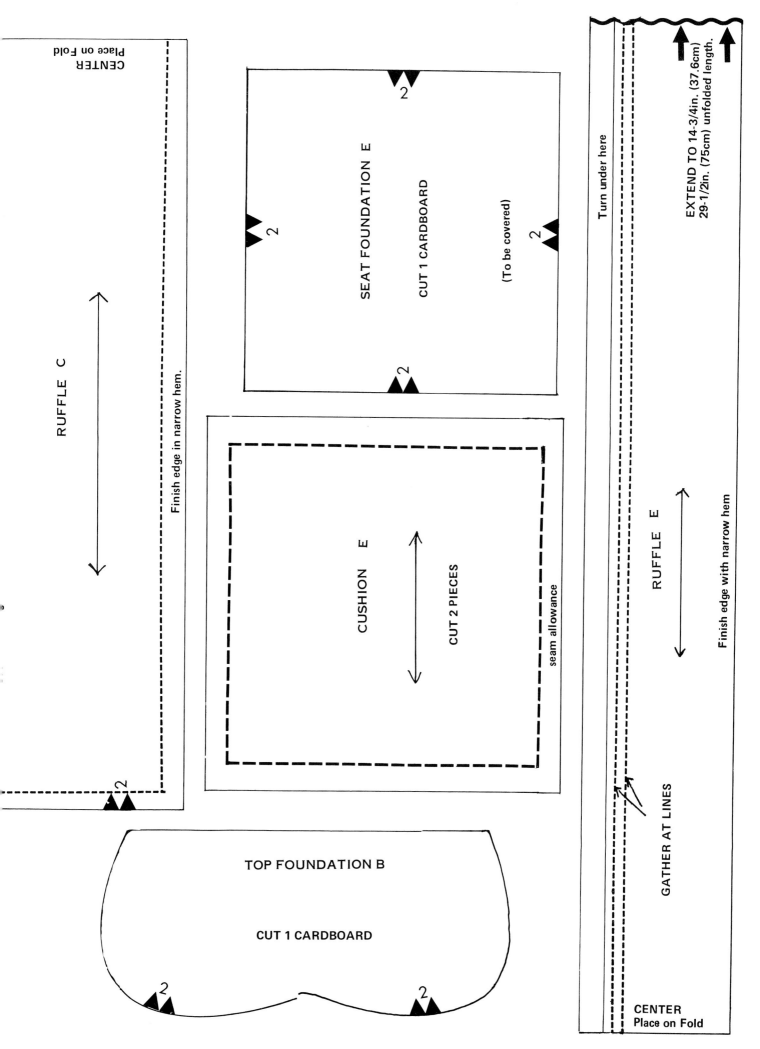

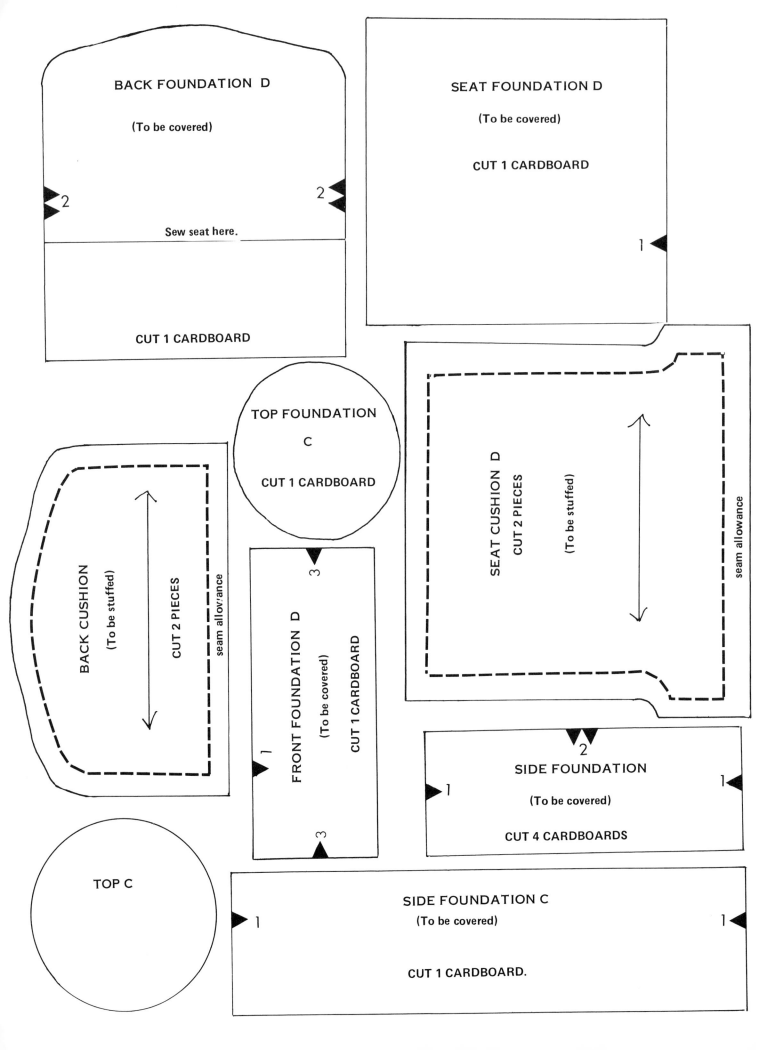

BACK FOUNDATION D

(To be covered)

2

2

Sew seat here.

CUT 1 CARDBOARD

SEAT FOUNDATION D

(To be covered)

CUT 1 CARDBOARD

1

TOP FOUNDATION C

CUT 1 CARDBOARD

BACK CUSHION

(To be stuffed)

CUT 2 PIECES

seam allowance

SEAT CUSHION D

CUT 2 PIECES

(To be stuffed)

seam allowance

FRONT FOUNDATION D

(To be covered)

CUT 1 CARDBOARD

3

1

3

SIDE FOUNDATION

2

(To be covered)

1

1

CUT 4 CARDBOARDS

TOP C

SIDE FOUNDATION C

(To be covered)

1

1

CUT 1 CARDBOARD.

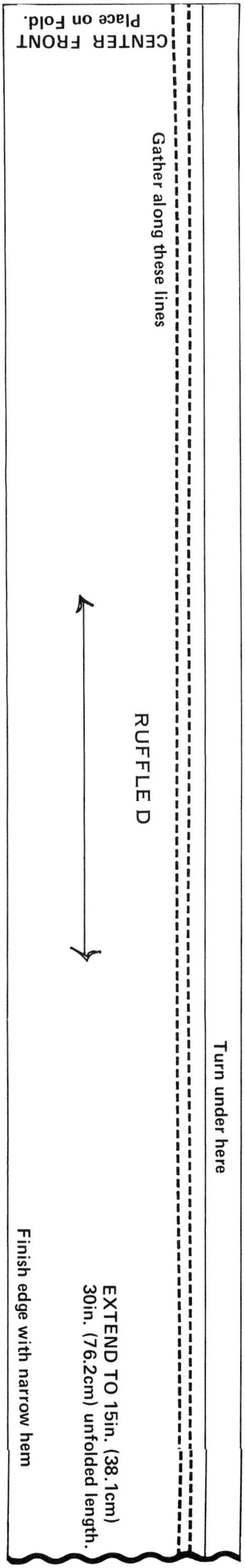

CENTER FRONT
Place on Fold.

Gather along these lines

SIDE FOUNDATION D

(To be covered)

Pad to this line.

2

3

CUT 2 CARDBOARDS

FRONT FOUNDATION F

(To be covered)

CUT 1 CARDBOARD

4

4

RUFFLE D

Turn under here

seam allowance

SEAT FOUNDATION F

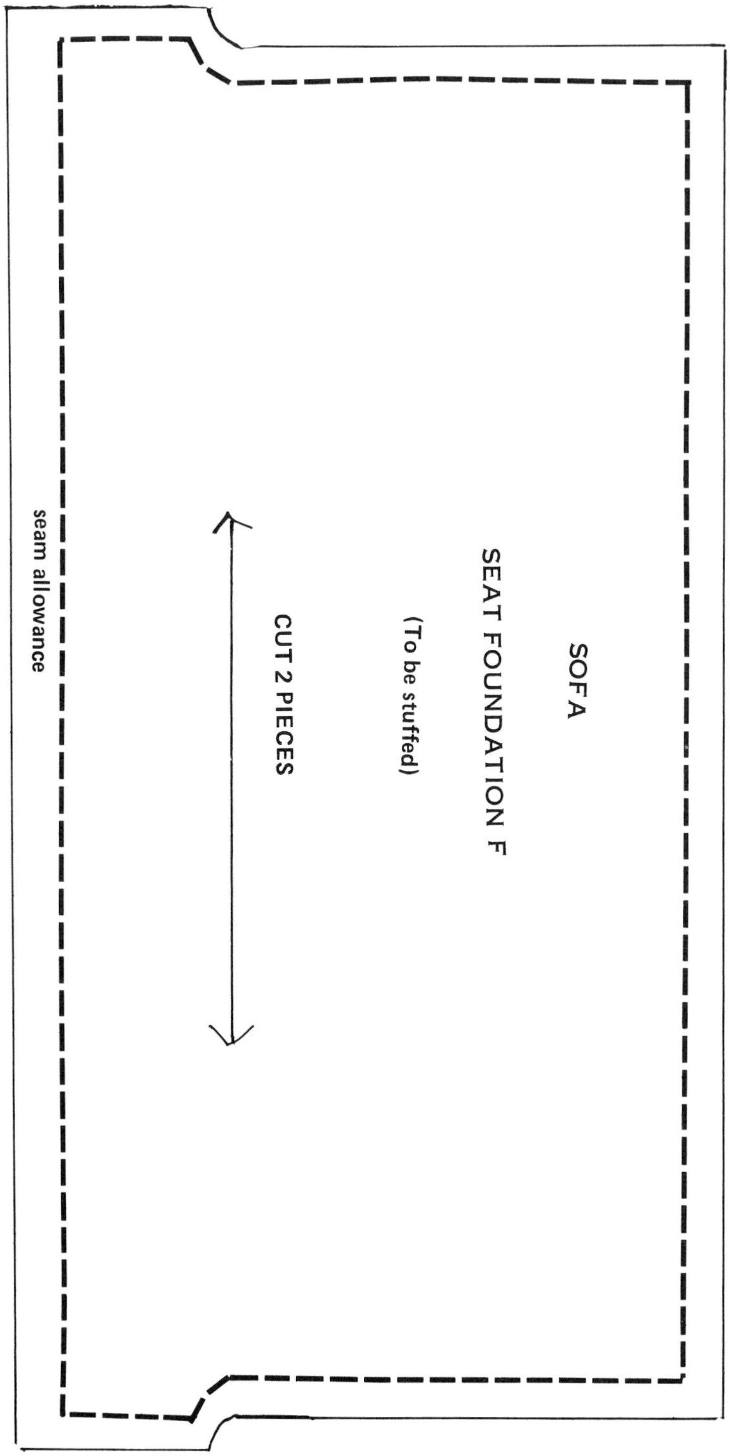

SOFA

(To be stuffed)

CUT 2 PIECES

EXTEND TO 15in. (38.1cm)
30in. (76.2cm) unfolded length.

Finish edge with narrow hem

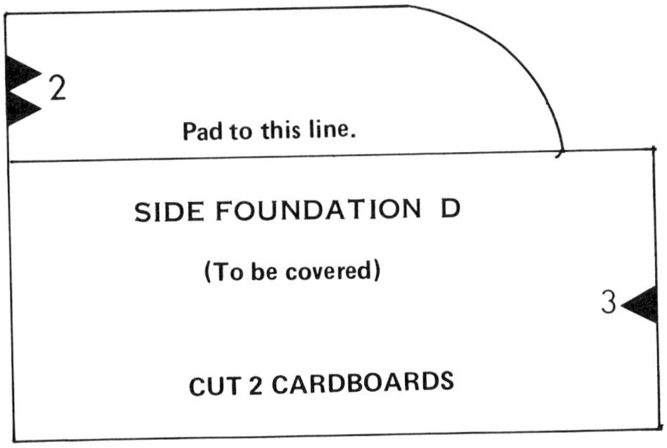

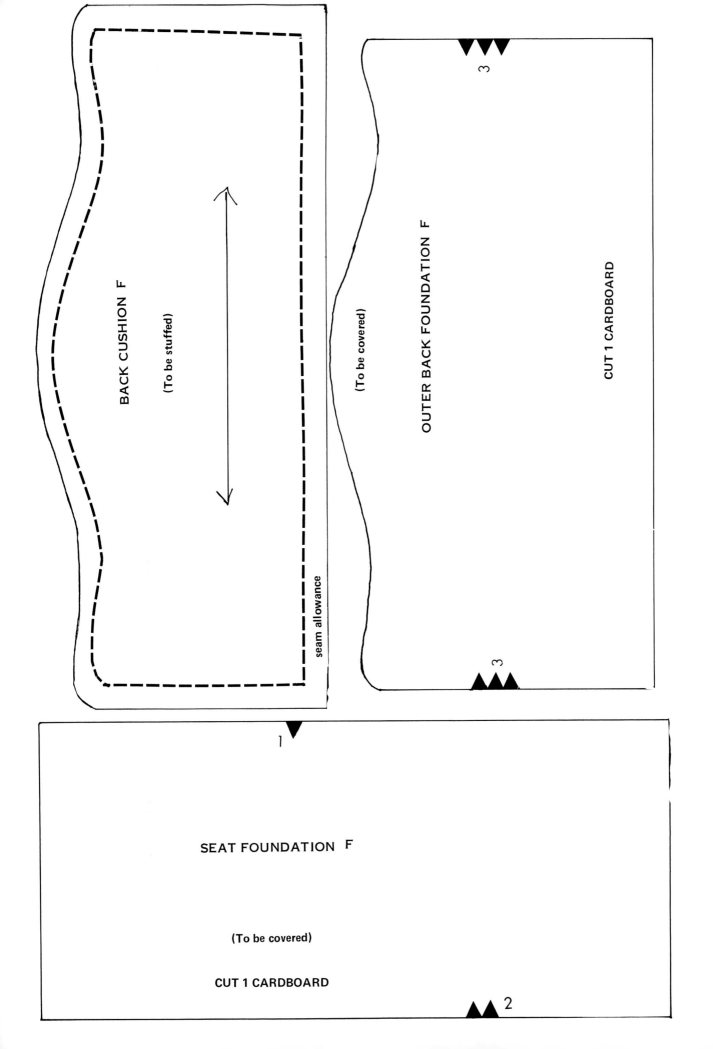

BACK CUSHION F

(To be stuffed)

seam allowance

OUTER BACK FOUNDATION F

(To be covered)

CUT 1 CARDBOARD

3

3

1

SEAT FOUNDATION F

(To be covered)

CUT 1 CARDBOARD

2

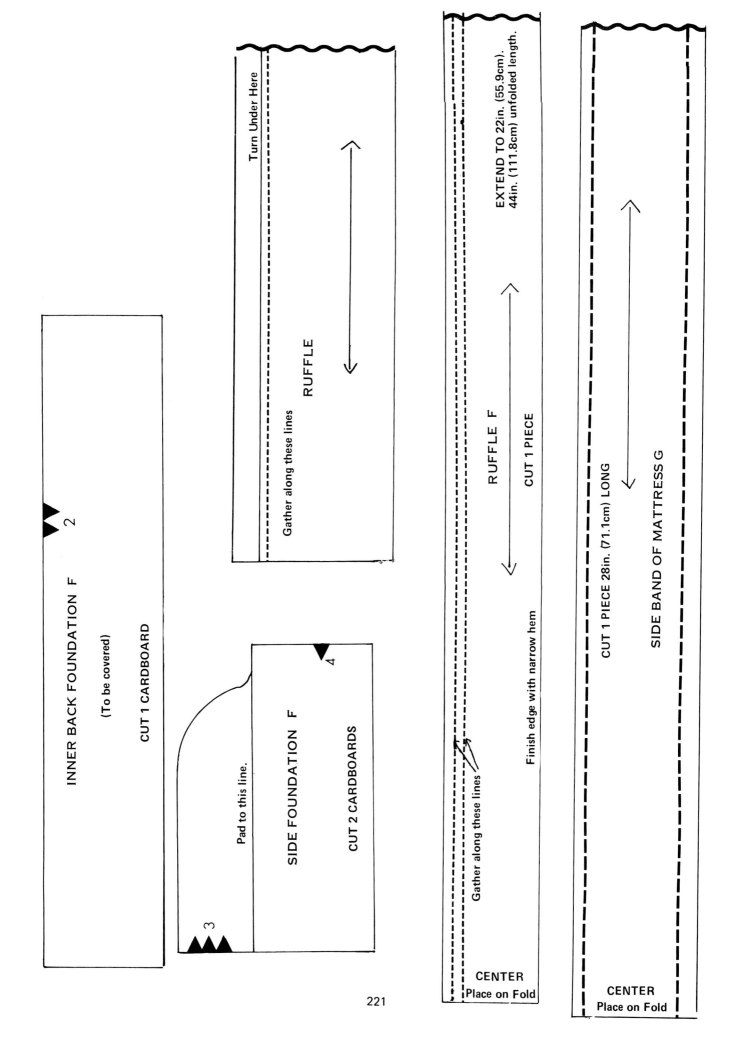

INNER BACK FOUNDATION F

(To be covered)

CUT 1 CARDBOARD

2

SIDE FOUNDATION F

CUT 2 CARDBOARDS

Pad to this line.

3

4

Turn Under Here

Gather along these lines

RUFFLE

RUFFLE F

CUT 1 PIECE

EXTEND TO 22in. (55.9cm).
44in. (111.8cm) unfolded length.

Finish edge with narrow hem

Gather along these lines

CENTER
Place on Fold

CUT 1 PIECE 28in. (71.1cm) LONG

SIDE BAND OF MATTRESS G

CENTER
Place on Fold

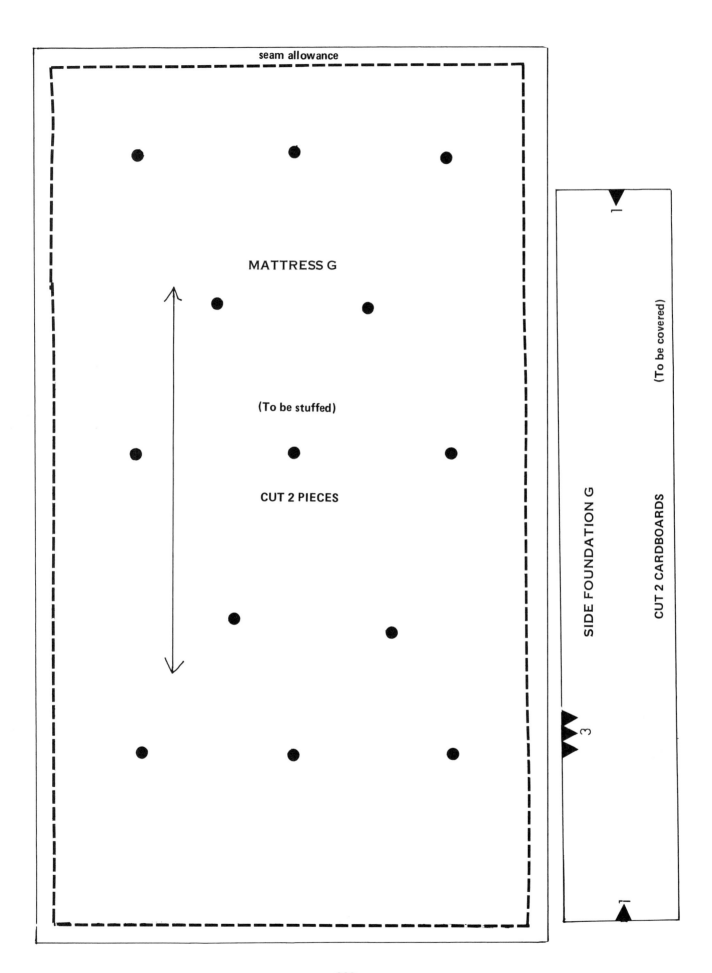

seam allowance

MATTRESS G

(To be stuffed)

CUT 2 PIECES

SIDE FOUNDATION G

(To be covered)

CUT 2 CARDBOARDS

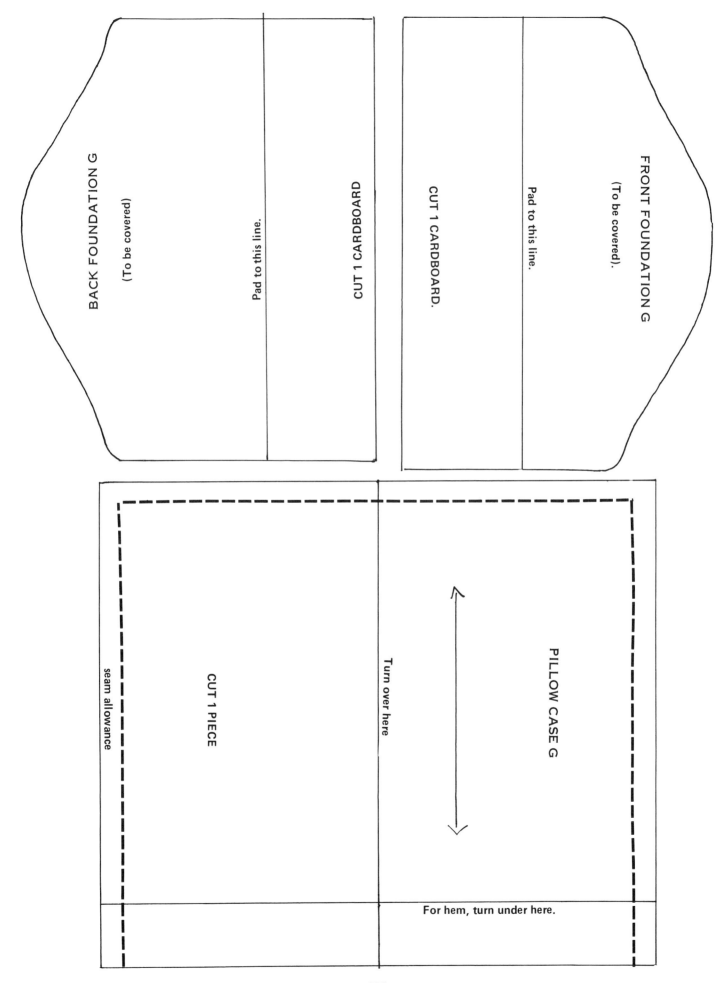

BACK FOUNDATION G

(To be covered)

Pad to this line.

CUT 1 CARDBOARD

CUT 1 CARDBOARD.

Pad to this line.

FRONT FOUNDATION G

(To be covered).

seam allowance

CUT 1 PIECE

Turn over here

PILLOW CASE G

For hem, turn under here.

223

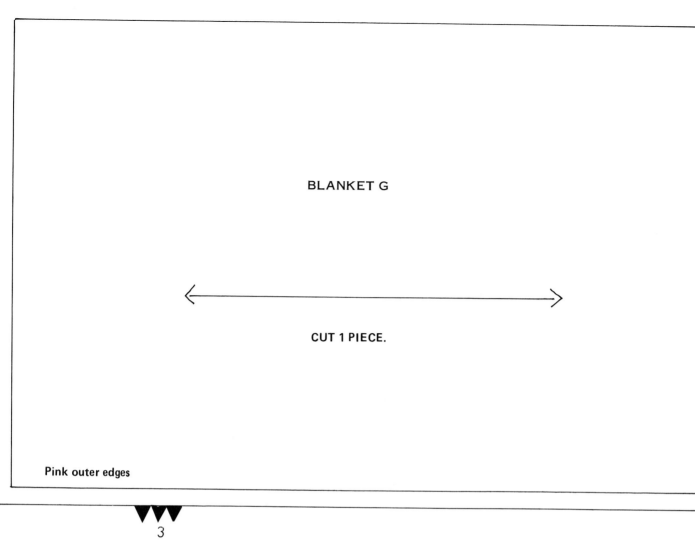

BLANKET G

CUT 1 PIECE.

Pink outer edges

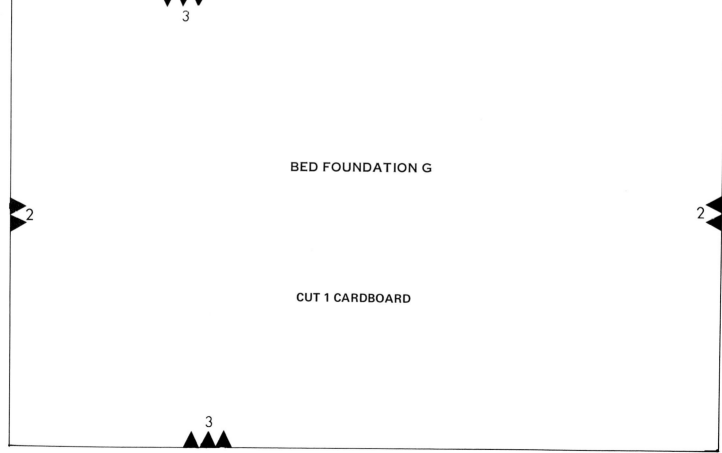

3

BED FOUNDATION G

2   2

CUT 1 CARDBOARD

3

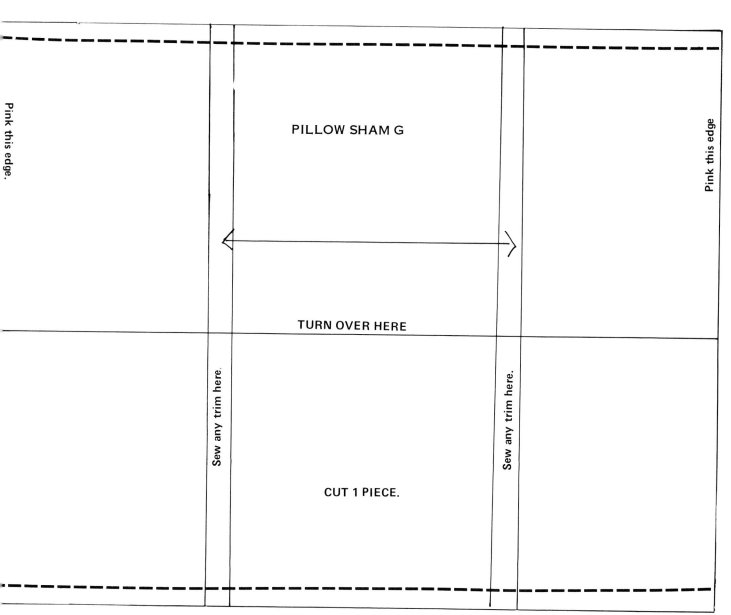

Pink this edge.

PILLOW SHAM G

Pink this edge

TURN OVER HERE

Sew any trim here.

Sew any trim here.

CUT 1 PIECE.

INNER FRONT AND BACK FOUNDATION G

3

1   1

(To be covered)   CUT 2 CARDBOARD

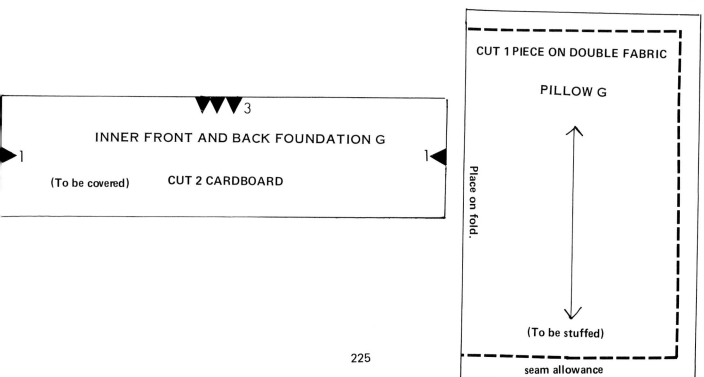

CUT 1 PIECE ON DOUBLE FABRIC

PILLOW G

Place on fold.

(To be stuffed)

seam allowance

For hem, turn under here.

SHEET G

8-1/2in. x 11-3/4in.
(21.6cm x 29.9cm)

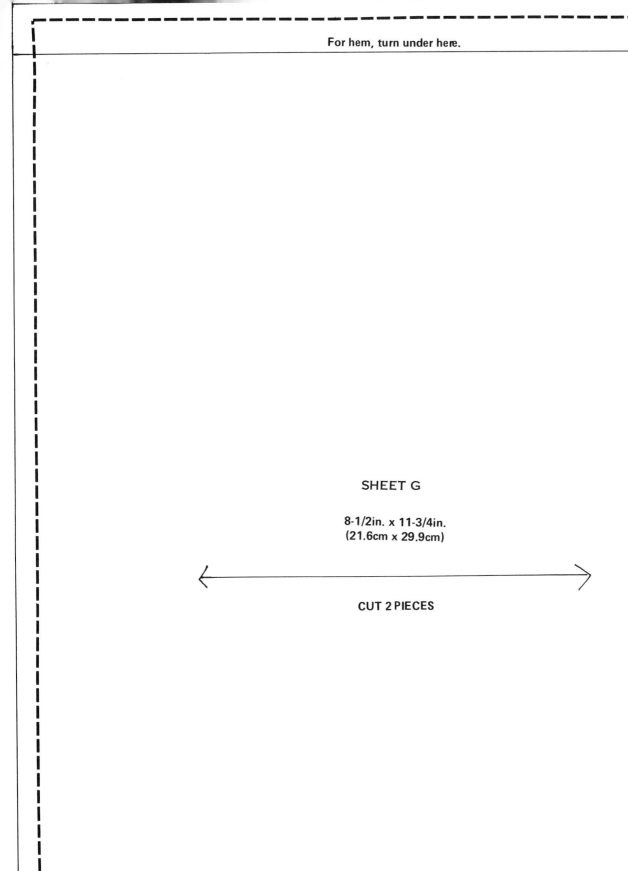

CUT 2 PIECES

EXTEND TO 11-3/4in. (30cm)

Extend pattern piece
·2½"

Sew any trim here.

BEDSPREAD   G

10-1/4in. x 8-1/2in.
(26.03cm x 21.6cm)

CUT 1 PIECE

Sew any trim Here

Extend pattern piece
2½"

Bibliography

GENERAL REFERENCE BOOKS

Hart, Luella, *The Doll Collectors of America Manual,* Boston, Doll Collectors of America, Inc., 1942.

- - - - - -, "United States Doll Trademarks 1913-1950," *Spinning Wheels Complete Book of Dolls.,* Hanover, Everybody's Press Inc., 1975.

Johl, Janet P., *Your Dolls and Mine,* New York, H.L. Lindquist Publications, 1952.

CATALOGS

Dennison's Gift Catalog, 1940.
Fred Harvey Gift Parade Catalog, 1939.
Marshall Field Gift Catalog, 1940 - 1941.
F.A.O. Schwarz Catalog, 1939.
The May Company Catalog, 1940 - 1945.

PERIODICALS

Adventures in Business, Vol. II, No. 47, 1945.
Glamour, December, 1943, pp. 74 - 75.
Independent Woman, December, 1944, pp. 370; 371; 386.
Playthings, March, 1943; March, 1945; October, 1945; November, 1945.
The Seattle Times, December 4, 1955.
Time, January 3, 1944, pp. 78 - 80.
Toys & Novelties, June, 1939; July, 1939; May, 1941; January, 1942; March, 1943; February, 1944; October, 1945; June, 1967.
Toy Trade News, March, 13, 1958.

OTHER

American Orchid Society Inc., Botanical Museum of Harvard.
Cooper, Marlowe, "Potpourri of Collectible Dolls", *Doll Home Library Series,* Vol. 12, The First, 1973.
Gifts from Disneyland, 1960.
State of California Dept. of Corp. Records, Sacramento, California.
United States Patent Office Records, 1940 - 1958.
University of Cambridge, Massachusetts.

Appendix

To Nancy and Les

FOR BEAUTIFUL MEMORIES

The magic of "Storybook Dolls" still lives

By the joy and happiness each little doll gives.

From Jack and Jill to the little babies

These lovely dolls wake such memories.

The sight of each doll made a tale unfold

And I loved them the more since I grow old.

Emotions were strong and I felt, as I smiled,

I was looking at them through the eyes of a child.

Though you are both gone, you surely must know.

Your "Storybook Dolls" we will never outgrow.

By — Ruth Thon

(Formerly a Bookkeeper for the Nancy Ann Dressed Dolls Inc.)

"SOMETHING BEAUTIFUL WHEN WE NEEDED IT MOST"

In the midst of world-wide chaos
Some little dolls were born,
They brought a sense of beauty
To a world that was weary and war-torn.

There were dolls for every day of the week,
Dolls for the months of the year,
Dolls to remind us of Fairy Tales -
Each one lovely and dear.

Nancy created so many dolls
That I have yet to see,
And if I had one wish to make
I would wish they all lived with me.

By Ruth Thon

SUBCONTRACTING

In spite of the fact that the Nancy Ann Dressed Dolls Company (company's name was changed to Nancy Ann Storybook Dolls Inc., on December 26, 1945) had its own potteries in Berkeley, California, and later in Stockton, California, the amount of orders for the dolls increased so that it was necessary to subcontract their production. They were first subcontracted to a firm in Japan and shortly this was discontinued. Later another subcontractor was found in Santa Clara, California. The business venture with this firm proved unsatisfactory and reportedly ended in litigation. The plastic Nancy Ann Storybook dolls were subcontracted to a firm in Emeryville, California, while the 18in. (45.7cm) dolls were subcontracted to a firm in New York. Mr. Bourla's dolls were subcontracted to a firm in Hong Kong.

TRADEMARK REGISTRATIONS AND DATES APPLIED TO VARIOUS DOLLS

Nancy Ann Dressed Dolls, a partnership consisting of Nancy Ann Abbott, Allen L. Rowland, and Frederick E. Anderson, a limited partner, assigned the following trademark registrations to Nancy Ann Storybook Dolls, Inc., 1298 Post Street, San Francisco, California, Corporation of California.

389,114	Sept. 22, 1941	403,240	Sept. 14, 1943	404,575	Dec. 7, 1943	422,241	July 9, 1946
389,115	Sept. 22, 1941	403,241	Sept. 14, 1943	404,576	Dec. 7, 1943	422,242	July 9, 1946
395,451	May 26, 1942	403,242	Sept. 14, 1943	404,577	Dec. 7, 1943	422,243	July 9, 1946
395,452	May 26, 1942	403,243	Sept. 14, 1943	404,578	Dec. 7, 1943	422,244	July 9, 1946
395,453	May 26, 1942	403,250	Sept. 14, 1943	404,579	Dec. 7, 1943	422,245	July 9, 1946
395,454	May 26, 1942	403,251	Sept. 14, 1943	404,580	Dec. 7, 1943	422,246	July 9, 1946
395,455	May 26, 1942	403,252	Sept. 14, 1943	404,581	Dec. 7, 1943	422,247	July 9, 1946
403,224	Sept. 14, 1943	403,253	Sept. 14, 1943	404,582	Dec. 7, 1943	426,526	Dec. 31, 1946
403,225	Sept. 14, 1943	403,254	Sept. 14, 1943	404,583	Dec. 7, 1943	428,592	March 25, 1947
403,226	Sept. 14, 1943	403,255	Sept. 14, 1943	404,584	Dec. 7, 1943	428,819	April 1, 1947
403,232	Sept. 14, 1943	403,256	Sept. 14, 1943	404,585	Dec. 7, 1943	432,208	Aug. 26, 1947
403,233	Sept. 14, 1943	403,257	Sept. 14, 1943	404,586	Dec. 7, 1943	432,812	Sept. 16, 1947
403,234	Sept. 14, 1943	403,258	Sept. 14, 1943	404,889	Dec. 7, 1943	438,495	April 27, 1948
403,235	Sept. 14, 1943	403,259	Sept. 14, 1943	409,267	Sept. 26, 1944	438,496	April 27, 1948
403,236	Sept. 14, 1943	403,260	Sept. 14, 1943	413,233	April 17, 1945	433,010	Sept. 5, 1949
403,237	Sept. 14, 1943	403,261	Sept. 14, 1943	414,597	June 19, 1945	512,668	July 26, 1949
403,238	Sept. 14, 1943	403,262	Sept. 14, 1943	417,245	Oct. 16, 1945	443,469	Oct. 25, 1949
403,239	Sept. 14, 1943	403,263	Sept. 14, 1943	420,077	March 26, 1945		

DATES OF FIRST CIRCULATION APPLIED TO A NUMBER OF BISQUE DOLLS.

January 1, 1937:
    115 and 142 Boy Blue
    117 School Days
    118 Mistress Mary
    128 Goldilocks & Bear
    153 Little Bo Peep
    154 Curly Locks
    155 Cinderella

    131 Elsie Marley
    132 When She was Good
    162 Princess Rosanie
    163 Little Miss Donnet
    141 and 178 Gerda and Kay
    187 through 198 Months
    143 and 145 Mother Goose

February 1, 1937:
    116 Red Riding Hood
    118 Little Miss Muffet
    152 Mary Had a Little Lamb

January 1, 1942:
    119 and 125 Alice Thru Looking Glass
    127 Merrie Maid
    250 Princess Minon Minette
    251 Prince Souci

January 1, 1938:
    120 To Market

January 2, 1942:
    122 Alice Sweet Alice
    161 Jennie
    252 through 261 Lady in Waiting

January 1, 1940:
    113 and 123 One-Two
    114 Over The Hills
    121 He Loves Me
    124,115 and 134 Lucy Locket
    144,161 and 173 Polly Put Kettle On
    157 Queen of Hearts
    158 Sugar & Spice
    159 Ring Around a Rosy
    180 through 186 Days of Week

January 1, 1945:
    122 and 171 Daffy-Down-Dilly
    144 and 172 Snow Queen
    168 Silks & Satins
    170 Rain, Rain
    169 Goose Girl
    175 Maiden Gay
    176 Nellie Bird
    177 Marjorie Daw
    178 Lassie Fair
    179 Daisy Belle

January 1, 1941:
    110 Little Miss Sweet Miss
    109 Little Betty Blue
    129 Annie at the Garden Gate

ACTUAL WORDING OF LETTERS SENT TO
NANCY ANN FROM "WEE COLLECTORS."

Dear Nancy Ann,
I am a girl of 12½ almost 13. I have 15 dolls of yours and think they are wonderful. I have seen Hollywood dolls and others but think storybook dolls the best.
I have been waiting for the dolls to come back. Please tell me when they will be come back.

Ann

Dear Nancy Ann
I'm one of your storybook doll fans. I have 22 of your dolls, I enjoy them very much. Yesterday was my birthday, I am ten years old. I got two dolls, A girl for August and See-saw Marjorie Daw. I have other hobbies, but I like my story book dolls much better.

Your friend,
Sally

Dear Nancy Ann
I had the sweetest wee doll No. 159 Ring Around a Rosy. I love it so please will you send the Storybook Dolls my Mumy say I cannot buy one owing to the doller but would love the book to see the dolls so I do love my wee Xmas present present doll sent from America.

Best wishes from a wee girl in Scotland
Love from Yvonne.

Dear Miss Abbott
The Cherry Blue Birds wish to thank you very much for allowing us to visit your factory to see how our Story-Book Dolls are made.
We all enjoyed it very much and loved all the dolls.

Sincerely
Sandra

Dear Nancy Ann.
Thank you so much for making such pretty little dolls. My aunt just gave me Little Miss Muffet to start my collection. I'm so thrilled with her and Mother thinks that size doll is the most fun to sew for. I'm hoping to get a bride doll for my birthday and anxious to start my collection of your colored pictures. Thank you for knowing the kinds of dolls little girls love.

Yours sincerely,
Patricia

Dear Nancy Ann
I love story book dolls though I only have one it is Princess Rosanie. if you are married and have a daughter she is very lucky if she likes story book dolls the one's I'm going to try to get is (I should of put three of them) are Cinderella, Queen of hearts and Beauty (from Beauty and the Beast) I would love to have a hobby of story Book dolls tho they are expensied and anyway were not rich and wer not poor Oh how is wish I was you're daughter (if you even have a daughter or if you even married) but if you are married (as I said before) oh how I wish I was your daughter! even if I do love my two brothers and my mother and father. well I really have not got much more to say (and I really said a lot to) well I guess I mus say goodbye now.

Your friend Lois

Dear Nancy Ann
I would like to learn more about the Season's Series of Dolls. Do you have a written story about each doll?
I'm 13 teen years of old could I sell these doll's for you?
Sincerely
Bettie Jane

Dear Nancy Ann
I am collecting your dolls. I would like to get little Red Riding Hood or Goldilocks, but I would not like to tell my Auntie in case it would be rude. She sends me the dolls because we have no dollars in Ireland.
I have Fridays child, daffy down dilly, Elsie Marley, Merry Little Maid. My Auntie sends me one every Christmas. I am sending you a snap of me but I am an Irish girl not a dutch girl neither is my brother.

lots of love from Lillian

Dear Mr. A.L. Rolland
Thank you very much for sending me the story book dolls. I like them very much. They are all very perty. I like them all so very very much that I could hug them so tight that I don't no what I could do. When I got them I was so delighted that they made me clean my whole bed room.
Well there is not much more to say so thank you again.

Georgellen

Dear Nancy,
Please write me and tell me how much the Storybook Dolls cost, Can you order these dolls? How much are the Dolls of the Month? Hope I haven't worried you but I want to know how much they are

Thank you
Golda

Dear Nancy Ann
I want you to know how much I enjoy your storybook dolls. They seem so real. I have seven dolls. A girl friend of mine has about 30 or more. I wish I had that many.

Yours truly
Nancy

Dear Miss Abbott,
We wish that you could realize how much we enjoyed our trip to your doll factory. Thank you for letting us go through it. We were all fascinated by the dolls and their dresses.

Girl Scout Troop #30

Dear Nancy Ann:
I just received the empty boxes for my dolls and I do appreciate your sending them to me and want to thank you for any inconvience it might of caused you. As there was no bill with them I will send you the remittance as soon as I receive it.
I think you will be interested in knowing my "Nancy Ann Storybook Dolls" won a blue ribbon of "Honorable Mention" in the doll show in New York. I really was thrilled as they had to compete with prize collections of prominent people. I would not exchange mine for any of them though, for they seem so real to me. I hope to collect many more. Being just 11 years old now I hope to collect many more.

Sincerely Yours,
Patricia